LAST DAY LAUGHTER

Welcoming the Redemption with courage, vision, faith, and joy

RIVKA ZAKUTINSKY
AND
YAFFA LEBA GOTTLIEB

Last Day Laughter

Published and Copyrighted © by
Readers Press
88 Parkville Ave. • Brooklyn, New York 11230

Copyright © 2017 by
Rivka Zakutinsky and Yaffa Leba Gottlieb

All rights reserved,
including the right of reproduction
in whole or in part in any form.

While this book is based on actual events, some names and identifying details have been changed to protect the privacy of individuals.

With gratitude to the women who gave us access
to their minds, hearts, and their prayers.

INTRODUCTION

we each have a G-dly essence.
reach deep. harmonize.
through our greatest, most intense,
most unique and deepest self,
we connect to each other, becoming one

Each woman of this book has reached deep, as deep as her personal exile, as deep, and a bit deeper, than the unique challenges she wills to overcome.

With inspiration from each other these women tap their G-dly essence, the root of faith. They persevere until they succeed in grasping their personal redemption.

Personal redemptions, the Lubavitcher Rebbe told us, combine to bring the cosmic redemption, the era of universal harmony and peace.

Women lead this redemption.

The souls of the women of our generation, according to Kabbalistic teachings, contain sparks of the souls of the women who left Egypt. These women had such strong faith that their bitter slavery would end that they prepared tambourines. They knew they would dance, and celebrate their freedom. They knew they would be redeemed.

Faith forms reality.

Today we more than anticipate. Now we watch, in awe, as the curtain of our final exile is closing, opening to our complete and forever redemption. May we encourage each other. May we delight as our personal redemptions herald the coming of Moshiach. Our joy is unparalleled, our joy has no limits. It is the joy of last day laughter--

V'tischak l'yom acharon...

On the last day, she will laugh.

--Mishlei

THE SET TABLE

Chapter One	LEAH	1
Chapter Two	AIDEL	7
Chapter Three	MONA	39
Chapter Four	LEAH	65
Chapter Five	RACHELLE	85
Chapter Six	REVA	113
Chapter Seven	LEAH	137
Chapter Eight	TAMAR	143
Chapter Nine	SHAINA	163
Chapter Ten	ORA	205
Chapter Eight	RICHIE	209
Chapter Twelve	LEAH	213
Epilogue:	WHERE ARE THE WOMEN NOW?	215
	SARAH'S END NOTES	219
ABOUT THE AUTHORS		223

Chapter One
LEAH
POSTVILLE, IOWA, MAY 8, 2008

5:23 a.m. Leah Rubashkin was very awake.

Today she would drive her sixteen-year-old son Moshe to the Mayo Dental Clinic. Moshe, born autistic, was challenged by bright lights, strange people, and prodding hardware. Sholom, Leah's husband, was preparing Moshe for the ordeal, promising him a special story when he returned.

The story would be a while in coming.

Leah was relieved when Moshe stretched out in the back seat and relaxed to music as they headed out from Postville to Rochester. They passed by their family business, Agriprocessors, the meat packing plant begun by Sholom's father, Aaron Rubashkin, nearly twenty years earlier. The elder Rubashkin, who lived in Brooklyn, had certainly left his mark here. A staunch follower of the Lubavitcher Rebbe, Leah's father-in-law had grey beard, deep smile, and snap. And a dream: to provide every American Jewish family, no matter how small or distant, with the best quality glatt kosher meat.

He found an abandoned plant in Postville, Iowa—a bargain. He picked it up, fixed it up, and Agri was born. Aaron rightly reckoned that the cows wouldn't come to Brooklyn.

But someone had to manage the plant. Who would go to Postville?

Aaron had his eyes on Sholom.

Sholom had his own dream: to be an emissary of the Lubavitcher Rebbe. As he told Leah soon after they met, he would go wherever the Rebbe sent him!

Sholom had a good heart. He loved G-d, and loved to say the entire book of Psalms daily.

Manage a slaughterhouse?

Aaron spoke. Agri needed someone trustworthy. Personable. Capable: Sholom!

Leah and Sholom discussed, figured, then packed. Yes, this could be Sholom's mission. Good-by Brooklyn! Good-by family, *shuls*, kosher stores, and yeshivas! Good-by community! And hello corn, potato and vegetable fields, and Agri! So what if the cows couldn't come to Brooklyn? Leah and Sholom would bring new life to Postville.

They invited other Jewish families to join them. Customs varied, yet all worked together, prayed together, taught their children together, celebrated holy days together, like one family. Agri put Postville on the map. Leah was proud of the community they had built.

Anyone who needed help knew they could ask her husband. Just recently a grief-stricken Agri employee, Mrs. Myers, poured out her soul to Sholom. The night before, her teen-aged son and three friends had perished in a grisly car accident. And now, on top of everything, with Mr. Meyers not well and no savings, they had to come up with funeral expenses! Sholom comforted her, took personal funds, and paid for it all.

Leah nodded to herself. Everyone knew they could count on her husband.

They reached the clinic in near record time. Leah parked, roused Moshe, and checked in with the receptionist. Moshe, eyeing the flat screen TV, grabbed the remote.

"CLEAR SKIES TODAY!" predicted the weatherman, his voice amplified to max.

"Moshe! Turn it down!"

"WE INTERUPT THIS PROGRAM FOR A SPECIAL NEWSCAST!"

"Moshe..!"

"Ma! *Look!*"

The room roared as Black Hawk helicopters filled the screen.

"Ma! *Look!*"

A wide-lens camera was projecting a war scene. Paratroopers carrying rifles, a caravan of buses with blackened windows, flanked by black SUVs, all swarming in a cloud of dust, in the front drive of...

"AGRIPROCESSORS, THE LARGEST KOSHER MEAT PACKING HOUSE IN THE UNITED STATES, IS BEING RAIDED BY THE FEDERAL IMMIGRATION AGENCY FOR ALLEGED HIRING OF ILLEGAL WORKERS. THE BIGGEST FEDERAL RAID IN U.S. HISTORY..."

Workers—*their workers!* Being led away in shackles! Leah gasped. The Feds had come to Agri.

Where was Sholom?

Obviously, she couldn't reach him now. He would be getting things under control as much as possible. He would show papers that their workers were *not* illegal!

From where she was now, how could she help?

Leah reached for her cell phone, to call Sholom's sister, Sarah.

* * *

10:11 a.m. Sarah was setting up the dining room tables, preparing for today's Tuesday Lunch and Learn. Her topic for the day: Redemption.

10:12 a.m. She was planning to discuss how the Jews' deliverance from Egyptian slavery became the template for all future redemptions.

10:13 a.m. In less than six minutes, her understanding of redemption would reach new depths.

10:14 a.m. Meanwhile, she had three minutes to plan her discussion of aspects of redemption: personal, national, and cosmic.

10:15 a.m. Sarah neatly stacked printed copies of today's studies on the buffet,

10:16 a.m. and put out the stemware,

10:17 a.m. and opened the door for Mira, who came to help with the set-up. Out came the flatware.

10:18 a.m. The phone rang. *Rubashkin* on the caller ID. It was Sarah's sister-in-law Leah. Strange that Leah was calling now. They spoke just last night.

"Leah?"

"Sarah!"

"Can't hear you! Bad connection?"

"Sarah! We're being invaded! *Helicopters, paratroopers, soldiers with rifles drawn—hundreds of troops—all over the plant. They're shackling the workers! Postville's a battle zone...*"

"Shackles... a what?"

"Federal agents all over! Sarah—pray for us! Please! Go to the Ohel..."

"Leah... I can hardly hear you! Yes, of course. I'll go."

The Ohel—the resting place of the previous Lubavitcher Rebbe, Rabbi Yosef Yitzchak Schneerson, and his son in law, Rabbi

Menachem Mendel Schneerson. According to tradition, when Jews are troubled they visit the gravesites of their ancestors, holy people, or prophets, and pray that in the merit of their connection to the righteous their requests will be fulfilled.

Sarah called her mother, told her gently. She would want to come, too. Their friend Reva Keter would drive them.

Meanwhile, in less than two hours the women would be coming to lunch and learn. Sarah called her friend Tamar Edelson to fill in for her. "I won't be on time... can't talk about it now. But please, look out for Aidel Lewis. She just moved to Brooklyn. You can introduce her, explain..."

Explain what?

Sarah, on her way to the Ohel, was no longer on the line.

* * *

Tamar stopped in her tracks, and wondered at her silent cell phone. Sarah had never left so abruptly. What kind of emergency was this! Tamar breathed deeply, and reached into her mind for an appropriate thought.

Think good and it will *be* good!

Yes, but what was *wrong*? If someone wasn't well, Sarah would have said so. What else could it be? What else could hit so suddenly, as though from outer space?

G-d does everything for the best!

Tamar did find some comfort in this. We can't see the whole picture, G-d does, and all he does is for the best. So what could she do now? Tamar turned her mind to Aidel Lewis.

Many women new in town drop in to Sarah's Tuesday Torah Lunch and Learn. They come for a good word, a good lunch, or just to meet friendly faces. Tamar was the first to learn at this table with Sarah, how many years ago! She had seen many women join them.

These women were often in transition, between locations or vocations, or just life situations. And the women faced transitions in different ways. Some stayed grounded, allowing change to happen, without changing personally. But others leaped, upgraded to a new level, new perspectives, with great personal growth. For this kind of leap, they need energy for the lift-off, faith for the flying, and trust that solid ground is waiting.

Tamar wondered who Aidel was, and what kind of situation she was facing.

She never could have guessed.

Chapter Two
Aidel

"You're really leaving?"

"I'm going... to Brooklyn."

"But are you coming back?"

"I ... don't know. I want to come back!"

They were weeping, tons of tears. Yet he drove her to the airport, on a highway of white ribbon, flanked with wide-leafed palms, unwinding, all unwinding, under an azure sky. He loved her, always loved her. Was she really leaving? Twenty-two years married, two great kids, why wouldn't she stay? They loved each other! Always wonderful! How was it she was leaving? Was she leaving? Wouldn't she stay?

They wept tons of tears. Yet she held tight to her ticket, as really she'd be boarding, checking luggage, here's the gate, yes she was boarding on this plane. Yes, here, here was her seat, here she sat and here she buckled, buckled, felt the pressure of the lift-off of the plane. She felt the lift-off and the pressure, the pressure, and the sinking, as she sank into the cushions of the fast ascending plane. And she was flying! Aidel Lewis, really flying, flying away! Flying away from Frank her husband, who was standing down below. He was standing there and watching, as this plane was disappearing, into heaven, as he stood there, standing all alone. All alone there he was standing, all alone he was hoping. Hoping that this plane was coming back!

And maybe it would.

Maybe, this plane would not fly forward!

Maybe, like a movie running backwards, this plane would now fly backwards! This plane with soft cushions would fly backwards in the sky! And land backwards, coasting backwards, on the runway to the gate. And all the people who were flying would unbuckle and walk backwards, and she too would walk off backwards—backwards, backwards, backwards—backwards and more backwards to be together with Frank again!

And if not?

For the plane did not seem to be going backwards. This plane was soaring forward, through the heavens, up to Brooklyn. And then...

Well, then, Frank could come to Brooklyn! He *could* come, and now he knew it, for he had just seen her do it, he could fly up to Brooklyn—he could do it, too. He could board a plane to Brooklyn, the very next plane to follow, He could follow her to Brooklyn, perhaps this very day! Yes, he could follow her to Brooklyn, he could board a plane and join her, and how thrilling and delightful if this trip could end that way.

He could catch a plane and meet her in Brooklyn!

He could, if he would. If he would! It was up to him.

* * *

To Frank, the morning looked the same. Sun was filtering through the taffeta curtains, glowing up the bedroom, glowing up the bedroom full of dawn. The bedroom was aglow like yellow daisies. Aidel liked daisies.

Aidel was like a daisy, her gentleness radiating like petals from a golden core, cheering everyone. Frank knew Aidel, knew her like himself. And even his friends, Bill and Mike and Ralph—and Ralph was like a brother—they all said the same thing. "G-d, Frank. For a woman like Aidel, anyone would be a Jew."

And that's what he thought, too. He was, after all, Jewish-friendly, liked Jewish things and Jewish food, and liked, more than liked, his wife Aidel who was Jewish. Of course, he wasn't Jewish, and his parents weren't Jewish. But his parents believed in G-d, believed in people helping people, and they lived like that, too.

Frank was up now, getting dressed, looking back, trying to find a clue in his childhood. He thought of his father. Everyone liked his father. On Saturdays, his father would be helping neighbors patch up a roof or sidewalk. And his mom? She was a stay-at-home mom. She liked to visit homebound folk, bringing them a home-cooked dinner. Everyone liked her, too. And she always had a lunch ready for those who'd stop by hungry. Everyone who knocked on her door became her invited guest.

And religion? Well, for Frank that pretty much *was* religion, his dad helping and his mom hosting, just doing good things. Good and G-d were almost the same word, his dad said. Good deeds, that's man doing G-d's work, and that's good. Also good to have a good name, his dad said. Words affect people, and certainly names affect people, so that's why he and Frank's mother called Frank, *Frank*—being honest, especially honest with yourself, is a good trait. Other names, like Rich, and Matt, and John—well, lots of good people had those names—but if you could be Frank, why not be Frank.

But be Jewish? No, no one in Frank's family was particularly Jewish, but no one in Aidel's family was so particular either. In Aidel's family, you'd find nice, refined people, open-minded people, who didn't care where you came from, just accepted you as you were. Frank could feel comfortable with Aidel's family, and Aidel could feel comfortable with Frank's.

Both families lived in similar neighborhoods, and got along pretty well. Frank's family wanted what was best for him; Aidel's family wanted what was best for her. And Frank knew that Aidel was the best and that's what she felt about him. They went to high school together, fell in love in college, and got married after graduation. Seemed that everyone they knew thought it was the best, the best match that could be.

Only Uncle Burd had a different thought, a thought that came out a few days before the wedding, during a pre-wedding family picnic. Uncle Burd found the beer and he was drunk. Uncle Burd liked beer alright—well, who in his family didn't like beer? But there's an art to drinking beer, an art to knowing when to drink and when to stop drinking. The men in Frank's family were very light in drinking beer, drank a little light beer and knew when to stop. But Uncle Burd was different, he drank serious. He drank serious, until he'd start talking out his words. Usually Uncle Burd was tight on words, wouldn't say most of them, hardly said any of them, in fact, until he had a few beers. Then he'd talk. And once the words started coming, he'd just keep talking, talking until he'd said all them out, and then he'd stop. He'd stop talking, and he'd stop drinking. He didn't need to drink any more.

So Aidel's family was all there at that picnic, her mom, dad, brother, some aunts and uncles. Frank's family was all there too, and everyone brought some choice food to share. Aidel's family brought bagels and cream cheese, coleslaw, and a fancy big platter of smoked salmon. Frank's family brought pickles, punch, potato salad and a big fancy home-baked ham. Now Aidel's family admired the well-baked ham, adorned with glazed pineapple slices and even cherries, and Frank's family admired the beautiful salmon platter, with radish and carrot roses, all framed with parsley. But as it happened, Aidel's family didn't much care for ham, just about the same as Frank's family didn't much care for smoked salmon. No one took offense. Both families had good hearts and open minds, and everyone just ate what they liked best, no hard feelings, just plenty to go around.

By the time they were getting ready for the pecan pie and watermelon, Uncle Burd had very much found the beer. The words would be coming soon, all of Frank's family knew that words would be coming. Of course, that didn't mean they'd be coming on everyone. Burd was discreet with his words, sometimes he meant them for everyone, but could also be that his words were meant for only one or two. Frank wasn't paying attention to Uncle Burd just then, but that didn't stop Uncle Burd from paying attention to him.

Uncle Burd came right up and put his arm around Frank, his sinewy arm, sinews strung tight between bone and muscle, leathery tanned skin laced with long blue-green veins and hairy with grey hair right up to the shirt sleeve of his well-bled madras shirt. Uncle Burd had a firm grip, and Frank did pay attention, then, to Uncle Burd's arm. Not a young man, Uncle Burd, but he was bone and muscle, sinews and veins, and strange, but he was family and he was guiding Frank now, away from the rest of the picnic, to the shade of a ginkgo tree. Uncle Burd motioned to Aidel with his head, motioned that she come too.

"Eh, Frank, I got something to tell you 'bout weddin's," Uncle Burd started saying. "I know about weddin's, how careful they all are on plannin', plannin' that flowers match dresses, an' dresses match tablecloths, very careful plannin' 'bout that. But it's the main match, the big match, I'm talkin' about, Frank, and you listen in, Adele (back then everyone called her Adele), and that match is, does the groom match the bride.

"So I'm talkin' 'bout that match—I've been drinkin' so I could talk 'bout that match—an' I'm telling you, Frank, in the Lewis family we've got this tradition that we don't marry Jews!"

Now if Uncle Burd hadn't been deeply drunk, he'd be offending some people talking that way, but now no one was listening besides

Frank and Adele, and they weren't so offended, not by Uncle Burd, so drunk.

He kept on. "Not that Jews ain't good G-d-fearin' people. Good G-d fearin' they are. Good, smart, an' sure got beautiful women, but in our family, Frank, an' I heard this from yer great Uncle 'Orton, in our family, we don't marry Jews. They're good, but they're diff'rnt. Diff'rnt like violets an' roses, diff'rnt like gooseberries an' peas. Diff'rnt like horses an' cows an' horses don't mate with cows, Frank. Won'erful people. But we're not like them, Frank, an' they're not like us. Wanted ya t' know that, Frank, wanted ya t' un'erstan' that, Frank, b'fer yer weddin' on Sunday."

"It's the beer," Frank assured Adele. "Uncle Burd has this problem with beer." And beer was what they thought it was, especially since at the wedding on Sunday, Uncle Burd, being sober, didn't mention roses and violets, or gooseberries and peas, nor horses and cows.

Adele and Frank were a beautiful couple, a well-matched couple, everyone said so, no one had any reason to say not so, or doubt it, especially not Frank, who never had a thought of doubting it, not ever, for the first twenty-one happy years.

Now that they'd be married near twenty-two years, Frank was trying to think this through. Was the floor dropping out from under him now all suddenly? Or had there been, for a long time, something creeping under the floor boards, something loosening up the screws, something prying at the joints, something getting ready for this all that time, this that was suddenly happening now?

He tried to think where it maybe all began. Not during their first years, for sure not. Jewish wasn't part of anything during their first years. Those years he and Aidel were just busy setting up the fine home they had bought. They made it nice and pretty. Then they bought their second car, for Aidel, and then came their two kids.

Hanna first, Louie soon after. And their first boat. But after that, about fifteen years ago, when Hanna and Louie both started school— maybe it was then. For Aidel—she was still Adele then—both children being in school was a major change…

* * *

Aidel, now in Brooklyn, thinking about Frank, rented a cozy little sublevel, perfect for a couple getaway. If Frank would be here… but Frank was not here. How long had she been gone and he still hadn't come?

So strange. They always did everything together. They always agreed with each other, putting the other's happiness first. He should be here by now! Wasn't she always thinking of him, and wasn't he always thinking of her? And not only thinking of, but doing for! Whatever she did, she did to make him happy! So of course, when she began to learn about beautiful little Jewish traditions, when she brought home tastes of this and that, she was doing it to share with Frank! And he liked it! Totally, from the beginning, there was nothing he didn't like.

So what happened, and how, and when?

Probably began when Hanna and Louie started going to school for the whole day. She remembered standing by the door, waving goodbye. Then when she came inside, she'd feel the quiet. A thick quiet. It muffled their rooms, afflicted their clocks, and morphed time into turtle hours, plodding from nine to three. Or it did until Rivki and Rabbi Mendy moved across the street. This young couple wanted to set up a Jewish preschool. They said they needed help. An assistant.

How perfect for Aidel! Aidel loved small children and could hardly believe that her dream job could be so convenient. And she was Jewish, not affiliated, of course, but Jewish enough. Frank thought the job was great—*A great idea!* Everything was just right.

So she began her new job.

But how could that have *changed* anything? The preschool was simply a little catalyst, which gently revealed a pre-existing Aidel—an Aidel that she had always been, but didn't quite yet know. The Aidel that she *had* known lived a simple, peaceful life, in a chameleon sort of way, imperceptibly blending with her surroundings. There was a peaceful harmony to that, and she valued peace and harmony. At the preschool, she felt harmonious, too. She just didn't feel so chameleon. Here her surroundings blended in and harmonized with her.

I open one eye,

I open two

I say Modeh Ani

'Cause it means thank you!

The kids at the preschool sang that little song first thing each morning. The tune was catchy, and Aidel began singing it at home. Then Louie and Hanna began to sing it, and Frank listened in. And Frank said, "Yeah? Why not! *A great thing—thanking G-d in the morning!*"

So they all liked the *Modeh Ani* song and they also all liked the Shabbat loaves, the *challahs*. Every Friday morning, Rivki would come in with a big bowl overflowing with challah dough. She'd say a blessing, break off a piece and then gave some to each child to poke and shape into their own small challah. Aidel made one, too. Shabbat challahs represent blessings, said Rivki. Blessings of fullness and trust.

After mastering the art of challah braiding, Aidel began baking her own at home. Frank loved it. He said there was nothing like coming home to oven-fresh bread! Aidel also began to light Shabbat candles on Friday night before sundown, saying, in transliterated Hebrew, the blessing to welcome Shabbat. Lighting Shabbat candles brings peace to the home, Rivki said. A unique kind of light.

When Aidel lit Shabbat candles, she felt something she couldn't describe, but Frank called it romantic. When he learned that Shabbat meals customarily begin with kiddush, a benediction over a cup of wine, he delighted in bringing home a new surprise vintage each Shabbat.

"A great way to cap off the week," said Frank. He liked going over to Rivki and Rabbi Mendy's for Shabbat, too. Their whole family would be invited for a nice Shabbat night dinner. Why not! They'd dress up, cross the street, and have a Shabbat experience with the rabbi and his wife. Beautiful, peaceful, lively, warm, happy. Shabbat.

Aidel remembered telling herself how Shabbat made her home seem complete. She hoped to keep these Shabbat memories forever...

* * *

Frank did like the Shabbat. Candles, bread, wine and Rabbi Mendy's lively Shabbat tunes. Not heavenly music, not earthy either, more of a good mix, gave everyone the feeling that G-d basically liked you the way you were. Frank enjoyed Shabbat.

Then Aidel had come home with another idea—the *pushka*.

A pushka, Frank learned, was a charity box. *Mitzvah*, another word that Aidel began using then, meant a Divine commandment. Helping others was a mitzvah called *tzedakah*. Not one of the Ten, exactly, but a kind of off-shoot, Frank figured. Louie especially liked this pushka mitzvah. He made his own pushka from a frozen orange juice can, and kept asking for little jobs so he could be paid with coins to fill it up. Frank devised ways to give Louie all his change, and enjoyed seeing Louie delight with each penny. When Aidel nailed a special pushka to the kitchen wall, Frank thought of his mom's kitchen, full of good deeds. Of course, in this neighborhood they didn't have needy neighbors, but Frank felt good every day putting a dollar in the box. The kids were learning to be charitable. Every penny a mitzvah? Good mileage for the money!

Yes, Frank had no problem with any of these little things. When Rabbi Mendy and Rivki opened their Hebrew school, and Hanna and Louie wanted to go, he sent them. His kids were already saying Hebrew blessings before and after they ate. Well, they might as well know what those blessings mean!

The kids liked Hebrew school, and even wanted to start using their Hebrew names at home. Hanna became Chana and Louie became Levi. Then Adele became Aidel. Small changes, but the kids were inspired. Chana researched great women who had her name, and Levi read up on great men who had his. As for Aidel, well, sure there had been great women called Aidel, but mostly *Aidel* expressed a character trait. *Aidel* meant beautifully refined.

And she was. Who was beautifully refined, if not his wife!

Levi and Chana wanted to know Frank's Hebrew name.

Frank's Hebrew name?

Frank thought, then answered. What he said was, as far as he knew, he was named after a mitzvah. Wasn't it a mitzvah to be honest, to be frank? That impressed the kids, Aidel looked proud, and Frank was happy, too. Happy to just be Frank.

As time passed, he gave his wife a lot of credit. She remodeled the kitchen so she and the kids could eat only traditional, Jewish, kosher food. They were very careful about it too. Frank was also careful. When he wanted to eat food that was not kosher, he ate it privately, in the garage.

* * *

Back in Brooklyn, Aidel was having dinner with her daughter, son-in-law, and their adorable baby, all together, in their tiny one-bedroom apartment. They were waiting to move into a bigger place. Everything in its time.

Rivki always said that, everything in its time. So comforting. As though everything certainly would work out in its time.

And looking back, as her children were growing up, things did work out. New adventures, new customs, new activities! Why not!

Aidel had only wished that Frank would participate more with their beautiful new customs and activities.

"Don't worry," Rivki had said, "We all grow at our own pace."

And Frank was growing. How excited he was as they prepared for Levi's bar mitzvah. "The best for Levi!" Frank insisted. "Bar mitzvah! *A mitzvah with a bar!*"

When Levi was about to start high school, he had a request, which he made in a very respectful way. He told his parents that he didn't want to stay in public school. He wanted, please, to attend a private Jewish parochial school, a yeshiva, in New York.

Aidel watched Frank as he considered the request. "I want to talk it over with your mother," Frank replied.

First, of course, Frank would need to talk it over with his friend, Ralph.

Good schools were important to both Frank and Ralph. They chose their neighborhood, a neighborhood with heavy taxes, because of its good schools.

And now Frank's son didn't want those schools. Heavy taxes, and he didn't want those schools! But Frank happened to have a local newspaper on the table, which said in bold print that in their own neighborhood high school—three students were caught in the lavatories, smoking pot.

Frank showed Ralph that paper. Aidel was hearing what they had to say—not eavesdropping, just hearing.

"What do you think of this, Ralph?"

"Not good, Frank. Not good at all."

"I think you're right, Ralph. And my son must think you're right too. He doesn't even want to go to this school."

"No fooling."

"Levi told me just yesterday. He's thinking he wants to go to a private boarding school in New York. A *yeshiva*."

"A yeshiva. No fooling."

"I'm thinking about it. I'm thinking that a school, like our school, might take the lead in math and chemistry, might even have a cutting-edge gym. But where's their bottom line?"

"Bottom line?"

"What I mean is, they're teaching, but what are our kids learning?"

"Yeah. Good question."

"You bet. And it seems that some are learning to smoke pot in the lavatories."

"Yeah. Seems some are learning just that."

"Right. Now I know people say you have to be open-minded. And I am open-minded, to some things, but not about young kids fuzzing up their brains."

"Nope. Not about brains."

"Yeah. Bill says so, too. Bill's got two kids in high school now, and he's saying that back in August he and his wife got called down to a high school guidance counselor family orientation meeting. To orient parents, you see. And their orientation was that *parents* have to be open-minded if their daughter wants to go to the prom with her girlfriend, or if their son wants to go with his boyfriend. Three proms they're having this year—one for girls, one for boys, and one for mixed. For all the open minds."

"Minds so open their brains flew out," said Ralph.

"Right," said Frank. "So when Levi wants to go away to a yeshiva high school, I got to think it through."

Ralph asked, "Well, you know any yeshiva graduates?"

"I know the rabbi and his wife," said Frank. "They learned in yeshivas. They teach my kids in their Hebrew school. Seems to me, their curriculum is mostly in ethics and morality."

"Huh. Ethics and morality."

"Right. Ethics and morality. And they teach as much by being as by books."

"They set the example, huh? That's good."

"More than good. That's how I learned when I was a boy. By example. This rabbi and his wife visit the sick, invite people over for dinner, and you know what? They teach about honoring parents. You should see how my kids *stand up* when I walk in. Like I was a king or something."

"No! Yeah?!"

"Yeah! That's what the rabbi teaches, and *he* learned it from yeshiva."

"Pretty good, Frank."

"Yeah. Pretty good. And he teaches there's One G-d watching over, who cares what *each kid* is thinking, saying—and even *eating*."

"Even eating!"

"Even smoking, I'd say. So I'm saying Hebrew schools make good kids, and a yeshiva will make good adults."

"Huh! Yeshivas." Ralph nodded. "If my kids wanted yeshivas, I think I'd send them, too."

That September Levi began yeshiva. Chana also went to New York, to study at a yeshiva high school for girls. They would not be far away—only a few hours by plane. Both children graduated with honors. Frank was proud.

* * *

Once the children left for New York, Aidel increased her activities with Rivki's woman's group, while Frank continued with his usual routine. Frank thought Aidel was happy, until she said something that must have been on her mind for a long time. She said she liked going to the rabbi's house for Shabbat, sometimes. But what she'd really like is to have Shabbat in her own home, with Frank, the two of them, with all the little details.

Well, he was glad she told him that. They always spoke openly with each other, and he was a little surprised that she hadn't spoken openly about this before.

And he told her, "I don't mind staying home on Shabbat if that's important to you. I really don't, Aidel. Look, I understood about kosher food, right? I even realized it wasn't right to eat not kosher food in the garage. If you and the kids don't eat it, I wouldn't either, at home. And Shabbat? Who says I have to go fishing on Shabbat! I can keep Shabbat with you. It's one day out of seven! A wife has a right to that!"

He was very willing. Aidel's happiness, the kids' happiness, was always his priority, so now he would make her Shabbat his Shabbat. He'd spend Shabbat with Aidel, and Shabbat time would be family time for the whole day. He'd walk to the synagogue and he'd contemplate G-d. He'd have any other day for watching the game and having a beer with his friends.

So he was okay with that. But he wanted to do it right. Shabbat had details, and isn't every important thing important in the details?

What's a wedding, or a building, or a business, without details? The more details you put in, the better product you'll get out, he knew that, who didn't know that! He knew some Shabbat details, like having the best food and wine and clothing. But there were more!

So Frank decided to go over and have a talk with Rabbi Mendy.

Frank never expected that talk to last so long. Rabbi Mendy had a lot of questions for Frank, very impressive how interested Rabbi Mendy was in Frank's desire to get Shabbat details right. Frank was only expecting a list of do's and don'ts. Didn't lots of people want to know these things? He expected that the rabbi kept the answers to these questions pre-printed in his top desk drawer.

But that's not what happened, not at all. Frank remembered coming back and telling Aidel, *A fine man, Rabbi Mendy. A man who understands! Asked me about my parents, grandparents, as far back as I knew. And we had a talk about Shabbat, how it's a special day that G-d commanded the Jewish people to keep.*

Anyway, the rabbi made Shabbat very easy for Frank.

The rabbi told Frank that he didn't have to keep Shabbat.

Because Frank wasn't a Jew.

"But—" Aidel had said. "You're affiliated with Rabbi Mendy's synagogue. You are practically a founding father of the Hebrew School. Doesn't that make you Jewish?"

It didn't.

She had tried again. "You're not affiliated with anything else. Isn't that enough to make you Jewish?"

It wasn't.

To be Jewish, according to the rabbi, all your maternal grandmothers, way back, had to be Jewish unless you converted.

However, as Frank told Aidel, he himself really didn't mind about not being Jewish. He'd still have commandments. Rabbi Mendy told him about the seven laws that the Torah gives to non-Jews. Known as the Seven Universal, or Noahide Laws, every descendant of Noah who is not Jewish is commanded to keep them. Rabbi Mendy told Frank what they were, and Frank agreed with every one of them. Believe in G-d, the Creator (Frank did); Don't blaspheme (Frank didn't); Don't murder, don't steal (Frank wouldn't, Frank didn't); Have and uphold a just legal system (Frank totally approved). And Frank also had a moral and ethical married life, and he wouldn't eat the limb of a living animal. Those were his seven, and Frank totally planned on keeping every one. He was a committed, family-loving man, who would keep the laws meant for him, while his wife and his children kept the laws meant for them.

He loved his wife and kids being Jewish, and for himself, he loved the Noahide Seven.

Wasn't that good enough?

* * *

It wasn't. But why wasn't it? Again, again, Aidel asked herself—why wasn't it good enough! Frank had his mitzvahs, they had theirs. What difference should it make!

And Frank was trying so hard. He really *would* continue to make kiddush for her on Shabbat day, but Aidel felt he might as well go fishing. Fishing was Frank's communion with nature, and being with his buddies was his way of renewal—just as Shabbat was a time of weekly renewal for her. She continued to go to Rivki and Rabbi Mendy's for Shabbat. Other families in the community were becoming religiously observant. Some even moved nearby. Rivki and Rabbi Mendy's Shabbat table was lively and full.

Aidel often sat next to Cara, a woman in her early forties, who was fast becoming more observant than her husband Marc. Marc, a reticent research analyst, came to the Friday night dinners, but on

Saturday mornings he drove across town, to work in his office. One Shabbat, the rabbi offered to make a deal with Marc. For one month, Marc should not work on Saturday, but instead join the shul crowd—as an experiment. Marc was to analyze whether or not working on Saturdays affected his bottom line.

Our sages, said Rabbi Mendy, assure us that we don't profit from money earned on the Sabbath. Even if we seem to make money, we won't have pleasure from it. We might have to spend it on parking tickets, doctor bills, and so on. Marc finally agreed that for one month only, he would not work on Shabbat.

At the end of the month, Marc had to admit that there had been no change in his bottom line. Rabbi Mendy grinned. Marc had taken a free four day vacation! How good was that!

Marc gave a tight-lipped smile. He added that an annoying legal case, which was to have been filed against him, was dropped a few days ago. But who says that had anything to do with Shabbat?

No proof, Rabbi Mendy agreed. But try Shabbat for one more month. Marc complied.

At the end of the second month Marc reported that his bottom line was pretty much the same. He made no less and no more than if he had worked on Shabbat. So again he had his free four day vacation. He agreed to a third month.

The third month clinched it. Marc received a new contract, nicely lifting his bottom line. Of course, he might have gotten the contract whether he worked on Shabbat or not. Cara interjected that it was time to spend some of that bottom line on the Shabbat retreat for couples that Rabbi Mendy had recommended. Marc agreed to attend the retreat, and to take on one more month of Shabbat observance.

Aidel, who always felt happiness when others were happy, experienced a rare emotion — envy. She didn't want to be Cara, of course, but she did want what Cara had: a Shabbat weekend with her husband. Instead, Aidel and Frank would watch a rented video on Saturday night and share a quick breakfast Sunday morning. Then Aidel would run to Rivki's women's Torah study group. And Frank...

Well, there was a men's group. But it wasn't Frank's group.

Meanwhile, Aidel, who was already observing the laws of Shabbat and the laws of keeping kosher, was intrigued by a third area of Torah law that was of special interest to women: the laws of the married couple, the laws which bring holiness into the intimate relationship of husband and wife.

Aidel let Rivki know that these laws fascinated her. She felt that she was ready to learn them and apply them to her own marriage.

Rivki told her, gently, that both husband and wife must be Jewish for these laws, the laws of mikvah, to apply.

Why should it make a difference?

But it did.

Little by little, Aidel came to understand that the way of life she was embracing, the way of life that fit with her and nourished her soul, did not allow her to be married to a non-Jew. She would have to leave her husband. And she did leave. But she hoped to come back.

She hoped Frank would convert.

* * *

His friends said it, kept saying it, till it echoed in his ears. *G-d, Frank, for a wife like Aidel, anyone would be a Jew!*

Frank felt it should be no problem. If being Jewish was like going to church—not that he knew much about churches—but his understanding was that if you put a few dollars on the plate, if you paid your dues, if you were a good neighbor and a law-abiding citizen, loving your fellow as yourself and listening to a sermon once in a while—if you did that—and he was willing to do that—well, what normal house of worship wouldn't say welcome?

She'd come back in a minute, she said. In a heartbeat she'd be back, if he became Jewish.

He thought it over, for a week. What he was mostly thought that first week was that Aidel couldn't be so serious about this. She didn't mean it. She'd soon come home.

She didn't. Well, maybe she needed another week. Let her have a good visit. Then she'd come home.

She didn't. She actually stayed a third week. That should have been visiting enough.

After a month, Aidel was still gone.

After a month, Frank felt it was time to visit Rose.

Rose's tavern, that is. He, and Bill, Mike, and Ralph often went to Rose's to talk things through. A good, quiet atmosphere. That night, he and Ralph sat down with their beer, until Frank began,

"I'm not sure I can do it, Ralph."

"Hmm. How long she been gone, Frank?"

"Near a month. Still can't believe she left. Can't believe she's gone so long."

"You can't stay together and just do your own things?"

"Well, I could, but she can't."

"Huh. Near a month. That's tough. That's serious. Well, get her back, be a Jew. I changed churches when I got married. No big deal and Beth was thrilled."

"I tried that. Went to the rabbi. He said I was fine the way I was."

"Huh. Said you were fine. Huh."

"Yeah."

"But maybe a different rabbi."

"Yeah?"

"Yeah. Maybe. Look, a guy in my office, Jeff Silver, is Jewish. And religious. Takes off from work twice a year to go to Temple. I'm sure he does what his rabbi says. He goes to the Temple a lot on Saturdays, too. Drives there with his wife and kids. But he'll eat out with us. Only has to keep as kosher as he wants to."

"Huh."

"Yeah. He invites us to his Passover dinners, and his Chanukah parties, and once he introduced me to his rabbi. And she's really religious. Nice looking woman—Rebecca was her name. Even when she's not praying she's wearing a prayer shawl. And she wears one of those whaduya-call-ums on her head—like rabbis wear. Yeah, a nice lady rabbi."

"Huh."

"Yeah! Talk with her. She's at Temple Beth Israel, got my wife's name in it. Call her up, the rabbi, I mean. I mean, if you're going to live as a Jew, you still have to live. Maybe she can help you figure out a way to do it."

Frank was pleased that Rabbi Rebecca cordially invited him to her office the following Wednesday.

Beth Israel was an airy building, built around a courtyard. Frank followed the rabbi on a pleasant tour of the majestic sanctuary. He admired the stained glass windows, the adjacent cozy chapel and the wing of classrooms for Sunday and Hebrew school. And next to the spacious social hall was a well-equipped kosher kitchen.

"Yeah, I know about kosher," said Frank. "Aidel made our kitchen kosher, and I never brought unkosher food into the house after that. Only ate it out. No big deal. Kosher food tastes fine, too."

The rabbi smiled. "It is one of our wonderful traditions. We do encourage our congregants to keep kosher at whatever level is comfortable for them."

"Yes," Frank agreed. "Why not. Nothing extreme. After all, I mean, a man shouldn't feel uncomfortable with his own food!"

"Yes. Do you have children?"

"Two. They're Jewish, of course. Everyone is Jewish in the family except me. And I love them exactly as they are. My daughter married a young religious man. They live in New York. They have a baby, named him Menachem, means comfort. I mean, they are very comfortable and happy with the Jewish lifestyle. My son learns in a Brooklyn yeshiva. He's happy, too."

"And your wife?"

"She's visiting in Brooklyn. Well, she isn't just visiting. She began to be uncomfortable, being married to someone who wasn't Jewish. My understanding now is that according to official Jewish law, we weren't allowed to get married in the first place. Well, we didn't know that then. I mean, when I married Aidel, I wasn't any particular religion. We didn't think it made a difference. And we really had a great marriage. If I could be Jewish we'd still be having a great marriage."

The rabbi nodded. Her brown eyes seemed understanding and knowledgeable. "A great marriage! Not everyone can say that, Mr. Lewis. Of course you want your great marriage to continue. And also, of course, there is much to be said for consistency in the family. Children, and grandchildren, feel more secure when parents share the same views about religion. Everyone feels that traditions hold a family together. It is an empty life without traditions. We do teach our children in both our day school and in our afternoon school about all the Jewish traditions. We are very proud of that. You can see for yourself. The children are inspired and connected and they draw pictures of Shabbat and holidays. Our little boys wear *yarmulkes*, skull caps, in class, and some of the little girls do, too. We don't discourage that. We feel that self-expression is very important."

"That's interesting. No, my daughter never thought about wearing a yarmulke. But she keeps Shabbat, keeps kosher, everything. Just without the yarmulke."

"Yes. Many of our women do that, too. Everyone at their own level, utilizing their own talents."

"Well, that's beautiful. How do you feel about converts?"

"We are proud of our converts, and we have many of them. You would be comfortable here. You know, Torah gives the convert a very special place. There's a special Torah commandment to be kind to converts. Our entire congregation has the greatest respect for them."

"I never knew that converts were considered special."

"Yes. It's a Torah law we study well. And we try to make the conversion process as enjoyable and uncomplicated as possible. We don't proselytize to convert people, but if an individual approaches us with a sincere desire to become Jewish, we do our best to assist them in their spiritual quest."

"That is wonderful of you. Maybe you could tell me exactly what I would have to do to become Jewish."

"We have classes, of course. We just started a new eight week series, and I believe this week is the fourth class. A very nice group. If you like, it's not too late for you to join them. Just read the material from the first few weeks, and try to attend the rest of the meetings. We do encourage our students to attend at least the majority of our sessions."

"Of course."

"Wonderful. So my secretary in the front, Norma, will help you enroll and give you the materials."

"Thank you, rabbi."

"You're welcome."

Norma was a pleasant woman in her early fifties. "Hello," she greeted Frank. "How can I help you?"

"Hi," said Frank. "The rabbi said that you could help me to enroll in the, uh, conversion course."

"Be happy to. I hope you don't mind filling out an application. It's not much, just to help us keep you informed. Name, address, e-mail, things like that."

"No problem."

Frank read the application, and noted that the fee for the course was twelve thousand dollars.

"We accept credit cards," said Norma.

"I see," said Frank.

"It is a little pricey," Norma admitted, "but the rabbi feels that becoming Jewish is a serious matter, and must be viewed as a lifetime investment."

In small print on the bottom, Frank noticed a disclaimer.

"Temple Beth Israel and the staff and administrators thereof are not responsible should the conversion obtained through them or their agents be not universally recognized or accepted."

"Sometimes it's not recognized? Sometimes it's not accepted?" asked Frank.

"We really have no control over the standards and opinions of other organizations who call themselves Jewish," said Norma. "Unfortunately, not everyone is as inclusive as we are."

"I appreciate that," said Frank. "I think I'd better find out how inclusive my wife is, before I sign up. I'm basically doing this for her. She feels that for us to stay married, I need to become Jewish. So whatever conversion I convert has to be recognized by her."

"I see," said Norma thoughtfully. "Well, we are well known for our conversions. However, our previous rabbi, before Rabbi Rebecca, was Rabbi Liederman. I worked for him for twenty-two years, until he retired. He didn't do conversions, and once I asked him why. All he said was that Kol Yaakov, the Orthodox shul, was better equipped for conversions, and if anyone came here for that purpose, they could rely on Rabbi Krause. Here's his number."

Frank, willing to consider all options, called Rabbi Krause and made an appointment for right after lunch. He decided he would lunch at the Red Rock Café. There he treated himself to the shrimp special—a generous platter of shrimp, accompanied by home-baked rolls, house salad, and a choice of beverage. Honestly, he liked shrimp. According to Rabbi Rebecca, he could continue to visit the Red Rock and enjoy their cuisine as long as he felt comfortable with it. Of course, he wouldn't go home with a platter of shrimp. No. He would not feel comfortable doing that. But he did feel comfortable ordering the shrimp special at the Red Rock.

Rabbi Krause, however, may have another opinion as to the comfort level of the convert. After all, if Rabbi Rebecca's version of conversion was not universally accepted, other conversions may be more stringent. Frank resolved to do his research. He would interview many rabbis, if necessary, to find the conversion that would meet the needs of both himself and his wife.

Rabbi Krause's shul was a modest brick building in an older section of town. When Frank rang the bell, the rabbi himself greeted him and invited him into a small, cluttered office. The walls were lined with old bookcases, sagging under the weight of fragile, well thumbed volumes, and the rabbi's desk was piled with books and papers. As he motioned for Frank to sit down, Rabbi Krause stroked his beard. Frank supposed the beard had once been red. Still wasn't totally white. The Rabbi's eyes were warm, brown, friendly, and tired.

"Thank you for coming," said Rabbi Krause. "Not often do people come to see me. Rabbi Rebecca works hard at Beth Israel. She teaches many people—people who think they want to be Jewish. Why would anyone want to be Jewish?" He said this with a smile. "Maybe you can tell me."

"My wife is Jewish. She left for a while because I'm not Jewish. We still love each other, and she'd come back right away if I became a Jew."

"And Rabbi Rebecca couldn't help you?"

"If not everyone accepts Rabbi Rebecca's conversions, my wife might not either. On the other hand, if everyone recognizes a conversion, she would, too. Do you give conversions that everyone recognizes?"

The rabbi nodded, still smiling. "You could say that those are the only ones I am certified to give. Tell me more about your family."

Frank told him and concluded, "Everyone would recognize that my wife and kids are very religious. They are happy and I'm happy that they are happy."

"To your credit. How did your wife become observant?"

Frank told his story, the rabbi listened and gently concluded, "You wish, then, to become Jewish to stay married to your wife."

"That's it exactly."

"And if you could stay married to her without becoming Jewish?"

"Could I? That would be great!"

"No. Your understanding was correct. The Jew and the non-Jew have different roles to play, and the Torah does not want those roles to be confused. How do your children feel about it?"

"My kids are the best kids in the world. I talk to them at least once a week, and they keep sending me the latest pictures of my grandson. They are planning to come down and visit next summer."

"And your work?"

"I'm a sales rep. I travel sometimes, but I'm home for the weekends and Shabbat. Of course, on the road, I don't have to worry about bringing not kosher food into the kitchen."

"Mr. Lewis, you are an admirable man. A loyal husband and devoted father. Your children will always love, honor and respect you, and with good reason. Your wife has much to be grateful for as well. We respect your desire to convert for your wife's sake. However, by the laws of our tradition, this reason alone is not sufficient to arrange a conversion."

"Oh, I understand that. I don't mind taking classes. And of course I'll pay for them. How much do you charge?"

"I very seldom give classes, Mr. Lewis. You see, a Jewish conversion is a deep and personal matter. You have to do this for yourself, not just for your wife. Also this is a spiritual commitment, from which there is no return—not in this life, not in the afterlife. You are still a young man. I encourage you to consider other options."

"Such as..."

"Consider not converting. You live near a young rabbi, Rabbi Mendy, he's called. Consult with him."

Once around the board, thought Frank, and back to square one.

* * *

Before proceeding further, Frank called Levi at yeshiva.

"Levi! How are you doing!"

"Dad! Just great! How have you been?"

Frank smiled. His son was going to be a rabbi, a leader. Yet Levi always said that although he learned great wisdom from his teachers, the foundation of this learning, the character traits of truthfulness and commitment, came from his father. Sons don't get better than that.

"Well enough, Levi, thanks. I'm calling because I have a question for you."

"Sure, Dad."

"You know, I'm thinking about converting."

"You are?"

"Well sure, I want to stay married to your mother."

"Of course."

"You know, Levi, it's so hard to figure out where I went wrong. You used to say that you learned a lot from me. Do you still feel that way, Levi? You've learned a lot more since I saw you last."

"I have yet to meet anyone more honest and true to himself, Dad, than you are."

"Yeah, I guess I learned that from my father. You don't remember him, but he was a good man. Simple. I mean, he was smart, but he liked things simple. Said there were enough differences between people, try to marry someone like yourself. And I thought I did. Your Mom is like me. We're both calm, friendly people, family people. And we have similar backgrounds—grew up in the same town, went to the same college, both from fine, honest, upright, moral, unreligious families."

"You had no reason to think differently."

"But it was different—it is different. Something really strong came between us, Levi, something strong enough to make her leave a loving, devoted healthy husband of twenty-one years, and a beautiful home, and a boat, and two cars, for what? She's living in a room in a basement! I think about it and I don't understand! Why did she leave!

"I don't want to be without her, Levi. I might as well be a Jew!"

"We'd all be happy, Dad, if that's what *you* want…"

"So I spoke to two rabbis. One has a conversion program, but it's not universally accepted. Would your mother accept it?"

"I wish it were that easy, Dad."

"You wish?"

"Dad, whichever way you go, you deserve to be authentic."

"The other said to talk to Rabbi Mendy."

"Sounds good. Let me know how it goes."

The third rabbi in less than three days. Three days of talking out his heart, three days that were not bringing him closer to Aidel.

"I miss her, Rabbi."

The rabbi nodded. He clearly felt Frank's pain.

"I miss her and I don't know how to get her back. I keep saying the same thing. I want her back. I'm even willing to become a Jew!"

"You've thought a lot about it."

"I did." He summarized his investigations. "And now I've come back to you. Have you done conversions?"

"No."

"Would you?"

"Well, they can be done. You have to remember that we don't look for converts."

"I'm getting the idea that a convert has to look for Judaism. Rabbi, for Aidel I'd be the best Jew this side of Moses."

"You're an honest man, Frank. Honest and sincere. But this is not about Aidel. It's about you."

"What difference…?"

"Look at it like this. Any non-Jew who truly wants to can become Jewish. At the same time, as you know, there are Torah laws for non-Jews. And those seem natural for you."

"Well, sure. The Noahide Laws. Those laws are just common sense to me."

"Frank, I think that when it comes to the Noahide Laws, you could be a real super-star."

"Yeah. If I could be Jewish on those, I'd be Jewish already."

Rabbi Mendy nodded. "So think it through. I'm here for you any time you want to talk."

* * *

Frank thought, and thought again, before he talked it through with Ralph at Rose's.

"I could stay married to her," Frank began.

"Yeah? That's good."

"Yeah. Okay. But I mean, theoretically anyone can be Jewish. They'll take anyone who... well, actually, I can't figure out who they will take! Like I told you before, you say you're thinking about being Jewish? They tell you right away: 'Stay like you are! It's great to be a good non-Jew!'"

"Well, yeah. Nothing wrong."

"Of course, nothing wrong! But I need to be Jewish for Aidel. So I went back and asked Rabbi Mendy. And then I went back again, and he told me a few things. I guess if I'd study for a year I'd get the basics."

"A year for basics?"

"Deep stuff. Yet I was feeling I *could* do it. I told the rabbi I would do it, for Aidel!"

"You would, huh!"

"I would! But while I was doing it I wouldn't feel like me. I'd feel like me trying to be something else."

"Yeah, something else."

"Cause something else is what I am. Like I'm telling you, Ralph. Being Jewish isn't about religion. Being Jewish is about a different species of soul!"

"Huh. Serious."

"Yuh. Serious. If I had a real Jewish soul, I'd say, 'Rabbi! Make me Jewish! Don't tell me no!' And when the rabbi says it's a one way street, cause once you're Jewish you can't ever be un-Jewish again, well then, if I had a real Jewish soul, those words would sound like honey."

"Huh. Got you forever. That's honey for you, Frank?"

"For me, Ralph, those words sound kind of sticky. Definitely more sticky than sweet."

"Well, how stuck can it get you? If you need out, a good lawyer knows how to break most contracts."

"Yeah. But this is a contract with G-d. G-d's got His own rules, and with this contract, it's forever."

"That's a long time."

"Ralph, I respect Jews. Respect them. Doesn't mean I am them!"

"No, Frank, doesn't mean that. I respect Jews too, respect everyone, but just looking at you, nope, no one would think you're Jewish.

"'Nuther beer?" Ralph suggested.

Rose poured out another. She knew Frank, she kept count, and she counted out one more. Another beer would be good for him. Of all the runaway wife tales she'd heard, she'd never heard one like this.

Frank drank some, put down the cup. "Ralph, you ever known me to be what I wasn't?"

"Never did, Frank."

"I loved Aidel. We seemed the same. Not the same now. She's not the same. I'm still the same. Can't be what I'm not."

"You gotta know yourself, Frank."

"I gotta choose: New life, or no wife."

"Huh. Some choice."

"Yuh. Some choice."

"Well... maybe not."

"Maybe... what?"

"Look Frank. Aidel's left. She had to leave. She had to be what she is. You couldn't help that, she couldn't help that. She's got a new life. Now, when you're ready, you could, uh, get a new wife."

"Huh. Huh! Only a best friend would say that."

Frank drank. No one to blame. Not himself, not Aidel, not G-d. G-d gave him a good life, and he gave G-d back like his parents taught him. His parents didn't say they followed the Noahide Laws, but they did. That's what they did and they were good honest people. They loved people, loved G-d, never held a grudge. And wasn't it true that the same G-d who made hard choices made beer.

Frank downed his. "Thank G-d!"

The worst was over. Ralph concurred. "Praise the L-rd."

Chapter Three
MONA

Tamar, still hurrying to Sarah's, tried to recall how Sarah concluded last week's session. She remembered Sarah saying,

"Our personal redemption begins when we..."

Why did Sarah have to rush to the Ohel?

Last Thursday Tamar had visited the Ohel, to pray that her youngest unmarried daughter, Abigail, would finally find her destined partner. Now *that* was a standard, pre-planned Ohel visit. Usually Sarah's were like that, too. Thought out, well planned, scheduled.

When Tamar opened Sarah's heavy, ornately carved front door, she found no trace of disarray. Sarah's elegant china and crystal goblets graced each place setting. Pungent, brightly colored salads—Israeli, purple cabbage, and baby kale—beckoned within easy reach from all points of the tables, subtle lavender hydrangeas peaked up from clear crystal bowls, pitchers of fresh water adorned with fragrant lemon slices -- everything was in order. Sarah's printed study sheets were neatly arranged on the buffet.

Tamar looked inside. Today Sarah was to begin the book of *Exodus*. The exodus of the Jewish nation from Egypt, Sarah had mentioned, was the prototype of all kinds of redemptions, from the personal to the cosmic. The Egyptian slavery afflicted us physically, of course, but spiritually even more so. Yet only forty day after we left Egypt, G-d gave us His Torah, the key and the pathway to our

G-dly connection. From the depth of slavery to the greatest of Divine heights – how was that possible! Can the human mind endure such a turnaround!! Tamar had only a minute to glance at Sarah's notes before the women began to arrive. Tova was among the first, bringing her tempting, just baked challah rolls.

"Sarah? She has a mission at the Ohel," Tamar had to explain.

"She got us a great substitute!" Rachelle, negotiating her queen-sized self toward an ample place at the end of the second table, radiated her signature smile. Meanwhile, Tamar spotted Aidel, welcomed her with a smile which Aidel warmly returned. Tamar scanned the room for Sarah's sister-in-law, Faygy, who would be the ideal person to introduce Aidel to the others, but Faygy wasn't here. Whatever had sent Sarah to the Ohel must be affecting the whole clan.

Not to worry. Aidel was already finding friends, and easily settled in.

Tamar greeted Shaina, whose father had had a recent hip replacement, Davida, who was enthusiastically endorsing a new kosher breakfast product, and Ora, whose Torah Teleconference chat group every morning (at six a.m.) had a hefty following.

As everyone made themselves comfortable, Tamar prepared to lead the Psalms. which were always said to begin the session. Women called out the names of those who needed healing, or livelihood, or children, or to be married—everyone had their list. Meanwhile, Levana slipped in, quietly beautiful, as always. She wore attractive clothing, yet one didn't especially notice what she wore. *Modest clothing doesn't call attention to itself,* Sarah had once said, *but rather it enhances the one who wears it.* Tamar asked her to read Sarah's notes out loud. Levana began:

Personal and Cosmic Redemption

Doesn't everyone have something they would like to be redeemed from?

For example:

a quick temper...

the clutches of yesterday...

the should-be's of tomorrow.

Or illness,

singleness,

childlessness,

demands of family, or friends,

business woes,

bad habits,

addictions...

Disasters—hurricanes, floods, earthquakes, war...

With personal redemption,

Through Torah learning, with depth and breadth,

And fulfilling mitzvoth, with faith and gratitude,

Loving G-d and caring for each other,

through humbleness, through joy,

we climb ever closer to our soul's Source,

the Source of our freedom,

our beloved Almighty.

And thus we seed the cosmic redemption,

abolishing exile at its very roots --

May we see Redemption now!

"Well, we're all certainly due for the big cosmic redemption," Davida's voice projected from the center table. "We have the signs, right?" She lifted her robust chin and waved an index finger. "We've had it all: earthquakes, floods, volcanoes, hurricanes, tsunamis, terrorism, extremes of wealth and poverty. And inflation. All the stuff that's s'posed to happen before the Messiah comes."

"Learning and yearning for Moshiach hastens it," said Tova, as she replenished the challah baskets.

"Personal redemption's no easy trip," said Helen, her voice taking on the intonation she had used when she had been the principal of PS 28. "Takes inner work."

Aidel sighed, no one heard. Inner work! Her marriage of so many years had evolved into one giant inner work!

Rachelle, delicately piling babaganush on a fresh challah roll, added, "From what I've learned, in the Messianic era there's *more* of every good thing!"

"There's honest self-work everyone must do," Helen reiterated. She took off her glasses, and let them hang from the copper beaded chain around her neck while she peered at the women in the room, each one in turn.

"Change what you can, accept what you can't." Helen personally relished change, and did not easily accept "can't." Before she retired, she, with G-d's help, had changed plenty. She had tamed the meanest public high school in Bed-Sty when Bed-Sty was still mean. She learned to know those halls well; she was out there, monitoring halls, until she knew each student by name and destination. Talk about names! When you care about someone, you learn their name, you know where they're from, and you're up nights thinking about how to get them from where they are to where you want them to be! Caring for those students until they knew they were cared about, that was her mission! Yes, change what you can—and you can! She cared, they knew it, and they knew that each young man in that building was to wear shirt and shoes and belt. In her office she kept a supply of ropes for young men who needed assistance in holding up their pants. "Clothes are for dignity," she told her students. It took time, but she took the time, until her students realized that they were worthy of that dignity.

They called her the Big H.

Even now she received letters from them. They told her how she helped them, how she changed their lives, how they never thought they'd succeed in anything, but now they had, and they wanted to tell her what they had become. Proud of them, she was. Missed them.

"Needs caring," Helen continued. She took a breath, looked around. She still had what to say, still had people who wanted to listen. "Self-work can hurt. But when somebody is caring, we can do that self-work. Free ourselves from our own self-imposed limitations. That makes for personal redemption."

"Didn't the Rebbe say that the next act of goodness and kindness could be the catalyst for what we've all been waiting for," said Yehudis.

Enter Mona, well groomed, quick smile, distinct jaw. Mona, a senior social worker at nearby Maimonides Hospital, struggled to find "appropriate placement" for patients whose health insurance ran out before their physical health kicked in. On Tuesdays, she came to Sarah's. She took her favorite seat, away from the main action, yet close to the tabouli. Ora was speaking now. Probably would put in a plug for her Torah Teleconference hour.

Lily sighed as Ora concluded that international agriculturalists go to Israel to study drip irrigation—proving that Israel was recognized for what it has done for the world. This recognition, she reasoned, was itself a sign of Moshiach.

"We saw signs of Moshiach in Auschwitz!" said Lily. "1943. We thought he was coming then!"

Mona focused on Lily. Platinum wig, well-tempered countenance, dignified make-up, aquamarine suit. Luminous Lily. Lily had what Mona called survivor's radiance. Live right, trump trauma, reach eighty, get glow. Lily reached beyond fearless and survived to challenge Moshiach: I'm here, where are you?!

Mona listened to Lily's story. Lily was tall, not frail, even at now. She had been fourteen years old when she arrived at Auschwitz, but a head taller than other girls her age, and strong. They let her live, made her work. She lived to be freed.

But Auschwitz didn't leave her. It focused her, colored her world.

Mona understood. She was also a survivor. She had survived the sixties, early seventies. Not like Auschwitz, of course.

On the other hand, not everyone who passed through that era did survive. Even in high school she had classmates whose brains had been "fried by acid," and whose minds became "spaced" by pot. Subculture stuff did them in.

Other stuff did her in. Oh, she did everything above board. *She followed the law, totally legal, did what everyone said was in her best interests...*

"In Hebrew, the book of *Exodus* is called '*Shemos*' which means *names*." Tamar was already well into the discussion. "Why Names? Why not Liberation, or Birth of a Nation?"

Names... Mona had her own touchstones. *What would the baby's name have been...?* A boy... or girl... gifted and G-dly... his insight might have cured insanity; her poetry might have inspired world peace...

She would have given a name, had she allowed her child to be born...

A story of so many years ago. And the law was, and still was, on her side.

Her conscience was not. *She never spoke of it—for how many years! Should she ever let her guard down? But how much could she say—and to whom? The women here were kind. But—she looked around Sarah's dining room. Who would understand?*

* * *

Time can carve out a mountain, rust an iron gate, yet some things time won't touch. Even now, so many years later, Mona could curl up on her sofa, sip hot tea, munch popcorn, and yet feel how, core deep, no comfort was comforting where she needed it most. Even at Sarah's she felt cut off. There was warmth in the lunch, and relevance in the learning, but how often did a word, a phrase, just catch her, and pull her back to another world...

> *"Don't do it. Don't believe it. Don't fall for the rosebud motif, the pale pink décor, the sympathetic, your-best-friend confidential counselors. Do not believe that any procedure is 'simple.' If you proceed, you will simply be haunted every day for the rest of your life."*
>
> Mona's Journal

I ain't alona cause I got ma Mona!

Mona! —That was *her*—!—everyone saying You are *the* Mona! She *was* the wake-up-and-pinch-herself Mona! And she'd never be alone anymore, ever, because now she had her Cliff.

Got my Mona!

That was Cliff singing, from his soul, with guitar, with twang, but that line rang pure, clear, sweet as rock sugar candy, melted in your mouth, had to be true. Cliff's twang and guitar, the icon sound of East Campus, becoming icon off campus, too.

Not alone...

And Mona didn't want to be alone, either, never did, always dreamed of being not alone, always dreamed of finding that someone who would make her feel precious, and not alone, forever. Mona's soul said that someone was out there, out there waiting for her.

...cause I got my Mona!

So many years later now. She didn't mention her age now—what a joke to think how thirty once seemed old! Now no age seemed *old*. Others *aged*. But her generation never aged. They *wised!* For so many years, Mona had been *wising*. If once she thought she knew the end from the beginning, now she'd struggle to understand the beginning from the end.

It began...

Back in the days when, if you wanted your denims rag-soft and faded, you washed, wore, and faded them yourself. That's how things were when she was growing up. At the university, she began to see femininity packed into those denims. Hurt, bruised femininity. That garment had a message: Sister, wear the pants.

Mona didn't buy it, never bought it, never would let her denims say that! She pinned her dreams on Cliff.

In the springtime of her freshman year, they married. An early, iridescent morning, sun beams bursting over the peak of Hilltop Park, with Elizabeth, her best friend, by her side, and the music of Cliff's band, and a blur-mist of Cliff's fans, all eagerly documented by local photo-journalists, there she became Cliff's wife. That evening Cliff played in an upscale coffee house, got reported as best performance ever, and their wedding night was after his gig.

She went with him everywhere, and times were good, pretty good. She kept up with her classes, mostly. Even her first visit to the clinic was good. She went for a pregnancy test.

She was thrilled to be expecting the baby that would be Audrey.

A nurse asked her: Was the pregnancy planned?

Planned?

It just beautifully happened!

* * *

"Sick again? What's the point of coming if you keep getting sick?"

She couldn't keep up with him, couldn't. He was traveling away, farther and farther, but she couldn't travel, had to stay home, had to listen to the music change. His music wasn't Mona now. His music was wine.

"Wine as sweet as the forest is deep—my wiiiiine!"

Cliff yo-yoed between his gigs, Mona yo-yoed between with him and without him, and the night Audrey was born was a without. Elizabeth was there, squeezing her hand through the hard parts, telling her before anyone that Audrey was a girl. Elizabeth brought her pink *It's a Girl!* balloons, and as soon as Mona caught her breath, Elizabeth drove new mother and infant home. Mona stood in the doorway, held a bundled Audrey, and surveyed her cavern…

Strangely still chaotic. Her apartment had not bounced back from the trauma called birth.

"You'd better rest." Elizabeth spread a clean sheet over Mona's futon.

Mona complied. Stiff, ache, hurt, hunger—all in unfamiliar places. She hadn't been coached for this end stage of labor—this coming home.

"You didn't have to be ignorant," Elizabeth commented. "Baby magazines choke with tales of self-care for moms. Look."

She handed Mona a splashy issue of IT'S A BABY!! Mona perused the cover: Fab 40 Must-Knows for New Moms! 10 Proven Secrets to Get Kids to Pick Up Their Toys! Eleven Essentials for New Dads! Two Views: Body After Baby! Three for One: Triplets First Year!

With no patience for numbers or exclamations, Mona sank into her futon.

She adjusted Audrey. Mona needed a shower and clean clothes, and the baby needed a bath and a change. Clean clothes. Was there? And food. Was there? And money? Was there?? She pulled herself together. Even if she hadn't returned to pre-natal, she still had nothing in common with non-student moms. She was a sophomore, majoring in "soc," with a term paper in woman's studies due in two weeks!

She couldn't even get up to make tea.

"Drink this," Elizabeth filled a tall glass with frothing double strength reconstituted orange juice.

"Too yin..." Mona protested, drank anyway.

Elizabeth shrugged. "Babies change you. You're a mother now—the quintessence of womanhood. Mother hormones are different. You could write your paper on that. Could, should."

Mona winced as Audrey pulled. "I'm not a bottle, baby!" Did babies have no mercy! Yet again she marveled. Nine months of pregnancy, a few hours of birth, and voila! A perfect baby. She shifted Audrey. Still stung, but tolerable.

"You'll toughen up in a few days," assured Elizabeth, who wasn't married, and wasn't even "going with" anyone.

"How do you know?"

Elizabeth shrugged, raked her fingers through her thick, damp, blond streaked hair, secured it all with a rubber band. "Sisters. Aunts. Friends. You know, life."

Mona punched her pillows, still trying to get comfortable as a mid-day sunbeam spotlighted her baby. A perfect strawberry-blond fuzzy little head. Adorable nose. Nice ears, borderline pointy, very cute, and close to her head. And an active mouth with strong lips... an amazing, miniature human being.

And wasn't she, Mona, also amazing! Without any coaching she had become something she had never even heard of—a colostrum producer! Special milk for newborns, who are angelic while they sleep. Less so while they nurse.

Surreal!

"Yeah. Motherhood should be part of every woman's studies."

Odd that it wasn't.

On campus, pregnancy was beyond odd. "Did you really *want* to get pregnant?" whispered the girl sitting next to her in Soc 204.

"I did," Mona asserted, though it wasn't anyone's business. She quickly learned that pregnancy and student-cy were a tough mix. For months nausea drove her from the lecture halls. Later, when she obviously wasn't just gaining weight, the interrogations began. Mona, who had never carried a banner in her life, eyed antagonists, stared them down. "What in life is more worthwhile than a baby?"

They couldn't answer, yet she felt their gaze. As though she were an oddity from Mars.

Audrey stopped sucking, fell asleep. Her little eyes squinted shut, her cheeks round and full, her tiny body warm and relaxed. A satisfied, well-cared-for newborn.

Mona felt totally vindicated.

And wouldn't Cliff be home soon? Home to share the miracle that was Audrey, and the wonder of Mona transformed.

Didn't happen.

Had he even cared about the pregnancy?

"Look, Cliff," she had coaxed him. "Feel, the baby—kicking."

"Kick, kick, KICK, kick, yeah, there's some rhythm in there," he observed. "like kick, kick, KICK, kick, KICK, kick."

He seemed happy, and before the end of the evening he had a new song. But pre-baby was not his focus, and their talk was old talk. Music, lyrics, his band, his gigs, his agent and what's for dinner. He was away often...

And he came back stoned. Often. Maybe this time he wouldn't.

He called that evening. Said he had tried to reach her last night, and the night before. No one answered.

She said she was at the hospital, having the baby.

He said, great, how was it?

She said the baby was a girl, named Audrey, the girl's name they had decided on.

He said great, and the gig was going great, and he'd be home in just a few more days.

He came back not seriously stoned. Brought gifts, for her, for the baby. Mona was elated, never dreamed he could be so thoughtful. The phone rang. Mona answered.

A woman's voice. "Cliff? Oh! Sorry!" The woman hung up.

Mona would discover that her name was Lori Wein. (*My music, my wine...*)

Meanwhile, Mona mused that Cliff had said that he liked the name Audrey. Yet

Audrey's my baby, now I'm a Dad

Sweetest little girl that could be had...

was not part of Cliff's repertoire. Oh, he'd bring a gift, win Mona back, then disappear, for days, for weeks, but time went fast. Mona was a student mom, with two years to go for her BA and something told her don't stop now.

Elizabeth helped her with Audrey, helped her find a part time job because Cliff didn't always leave her cash enough for the week, or the month. Mona was a working student mom now, and she was waking up feeling nauseous.

She got up anyway, went to classes anyway, went to work. Any way. Audrey came in a baby sling. They wrapped themselves in a thick, soft burgundy poncho, and sat near the back of the lecture hall. Mona took notes while Audrey slept.

Cliff still gone, Mona borrowed money to cover rent. Debt, maybe, was making her nauseous? Maybe, said her doctor, who insisted on a pregnancy test. Lo and behold.

Another baby?

Another baby, and Audrey—by herself?

She had tried to concoct that Cliff really cared about Audrey. Or would come to care. Because possibly he just didn't relate well to newborns. Or possibly he just didn't relate well to babies. He also was not relating well to Mona. He was home less and less, and stoned more and more.

The very next day Cliff was home again, with new promises, new stories and new songs.

So easy. So easy to believe him, the father of her child.

But two? She just couldn't.

The logical and only step Mona could think of was to revisit the clinic.

The clinic was a new building on campus, nicely endowed. Poised above the entrance was a reassuring logo, a graceful, feminine, long stemmed, pale pink rosebud, gliding on its side, with its beautiful, full tip pointing upward. The logo promised beauty, femininity, and future. And the clinic's literature promised counselors who were confidential, understanding and supportive. Mona poured her heart out to Tammy.

Tammy's wide hazel eyes were flecked with green. She wore a soft pale rose wool sweater and a full pastel rose plaid skirt, long until her sandals, which she wore over thick rose woolen socks. Her golden hair fell in zigzag waves over her shoulders, across her back. Noticing Tammy's every detail helped Mona not think about why she had come to the clinic.

Tammy handed her a flyer stating that all that transpired here would remain confidential. Not a word would whisper beyond the five by six foot cubicle that was Tammy's office, not a sound would penetrate these friendly walls where an adorable pink wall calendar announced the fourteenth of February with heart-shaped deep pink lace.

"You're very early," Tammy said with reassurance and understanding. She encouraged Mona to make an informed choice, and to do what would be for her ultimate benefit in the future. She could explore various options. Fortunately, she was still so very early that a very minimal procedure was a viable option to explore. *So simple. Practically just a D and C.* Tammy arranged the appointment, conveniently soon.

What future? Yet Mona kept the appointment for the simple procedure. What else could she do?

She arrived punctually, early in the morning, without breakfast. Sunlight streamed through the windows, bathing the room with palest rose-petal pink. A clinic designed to be comforting. She tried to feel comforted. Here was an isle of refuge, a calm retreat, a haven from life's raging storms.

It was not. Although the procedure went smoothly, Mona felt beyond sick, beyond weak, and beyond anger. Waves of pain, bewilderment and frustration, raged, relented, raged again.

Vulnerable, was what she was. Weak, was what she was. And empty! She went home, nursed Audrey, and wondered at her guilt. Why only now, did she realize her decisions reached beyond herself! Audrey could have had a sibling...

A child could have been born!

But two babies? How could she! She had reasoned that she had done what was best for everyone! Why was she crying? She distracted herself with a newspaper.

Headlines: *Baby Abandoned in Rubbish Heap.*

She retched until her insides seemed to have abandoned her as well.

* * *

Mona didn't get it. She couldn't understand her bewilderment, her rollercoaster emotions, her frustration. She resolved to focus on her Audrey, her treasure, and to live from moment to moment. Classes. Babysitting exchanges. Tuna sandwich. Nurse. Homework. Sleep. Again, and again, and again, and she passed the semester.

One morning she realized that Cliff hadn't been home for two months. She remembered the first time he had been away one night. What a scaredy-cat she had been.

Elizabeth stopped by. "You seem to be managing without him," she observed.

"Do I have a choice?" Mona countered.

"You have ability and capability," Elizabeth declared. "Guts and strength. Didn't think you were the type."

"I'm not just me."

"The lioness roars. What's your next move?"

"To finish my degree. I'll be a social worker. And I'll be Audrey's mother."

"And...?"

"And I won't be Cliff's wife." She didn't believe it till she heard herself say it.

"Bravo."

"He's not a father to Audrey. He's not a husband to me. I've faced it."

"If you're staying here, change the locks."

Mona watched Mona-the-strong do all the necessaries. Locksmith, restraining order, divorce. Demanded alimony, demanded child-support.

On paper she got it all.

Did *she* do that? *How* did *she* do that?! Stunned, Mona ate a slice of pizza, and slept soundly until she woke up for her nine o'clock class. Cliff had meekly requested visiting privileges, then took off for the west coast. Mona would never hear from him again.

* * *

Years later.

Mona had moved to Crown Heights. She came when the rent was still cheap, found an apartment, cleaned it, cluttered it, and so the years flew by. Audrey became Aviva, married Aaron, multiplied into Aviva, Aaron, Avi, Aliza, Ahuva, and Ariel, and they all visited often. Toys, child-art, and baby photos mingled with Mona's own jumble of stuff. This was her retreat after a long day's toil in the hospital's social work office.

Mona was well qualified. With student loans and scholarships she earned all the degrees before Audrey turned eight, and one door opened the next. New place, new job, new contacts, new friends. Away from memories.

During the years when Mona earned her degrees, Audrey spent time with the Lainer family. There she noted that some mothers, such as Naomi Lainer, stayed at home and made a home.

"You don't work?" Audrey had questioned.

Naomi replied, "I am working. My home is my work. I take care of my children Esti, Sarah, and Josh."

"And me?" asked Audrey.

"Sure. You, too."

I'm going to do that, Audrey decided.

It's cute when a six-year-old says, "I want to be a Mommy." Is it less appealing years later when she wants to write her sixth grade "career" paper on becoming a "Mother/Homemaker"?

"You mean Home Economist?" Ms. Garfield asked.

"No. I mean Mother and Homemaker. Full time."

"I'm not sure that qualifies as a career."

"Then I don't want a career."

"You want to be a government parasite?"

"I want to be a wife and mother."

"There is no curriculum for that."

"I'll make one!"

When the school principal called Mona, Mona suggested that while certainly no one should be forced into an occupation, perhaps wife/mother/homemaker, without the technicalities of "home-economist," could be an option. The reply: "Perhaps in a slower track! But Audrey has always been an excellent student!"

"Then let her design the curriculum and teach the course."

"I see where the girl gets her chutzpah."

What Audrey finally wrote was, "In Defense of a Career as a Mother and Homemaker," which despite its excellence earned her a B-, an insult which fueled her resolve to not swerve from her chosen path.

Mona wondered how many of Audrey's classmates entered and succeeded in the profession they chose in sixth grade.

Would her unborn child have been as remarkable as Audrey?

Yes, would have been.

At that time, Audrey was eleven. Mona could still have had more children...

Of course, she would first have to trust someone enough to marry him.

Easier to concentrate on Audrey.

Young Audrey absorbed other things from Naomi's home, including the word "Shabbat." One week, Naomi invited Mona and Audrey for a Friday night Shabbat dinner.

Mona remembered something about Shabbat candles. Her grandmother lit them because *her* grandmother lit them. Mona's mother did not light, but Audrey wanted Shabbat. So they went.

Mona was relieved to find congenial people, pleasant conversation, and delicious food. She enjoyed eating a dinner she didn't have to cook, and was happy to see Audrey so animated.

"Mona, this child has personality!" enthused Naomi. "How do you raise a child to be so outgoing?"

Mona shrugged, pleased. "Probably she was born like that."

"Maybe, but you must encourage her, putting her into a lot of social situations."

"I guess."

An enjoyable evening. And Mona was invited back the next week.

"But what does Naomi get out of it?" Mona asked Erica, another guest. "I mean, of course I'm coming back. I got fed, I got child care. And I'm taking advantage of her hospitality! For me it's survival. But what's in it for her?"

"Well, maybe some people are not totally stressed out. Maybe some people like helping other people."

"Admirable. Wonder if I'll ever reach doing that."

"Mona, you want it, you'll get it."

* * *

They not only became "regulars," but they began to sleep over Friday night, to enjoy a "full" Shabbat. Friday nights and Saturdays began to mean Naomi and Larry's. Naomi gave Audrey a book about a Shabbat fish, and gave Mona a book about Shabbat.

Three weeks later, Erica observed that Mona was essentially "keeping Shabbat."

"Huh?"

"Didn't you read the Shabbat book?"

"Just the first line: 'Just as the Jewish people keep the Shabbat, Shabbat keeps the Jewish people.'"

"Well, looks like you're keeping it."

"Looks like Shabbat keeps me—sane and in one piece. Yes, at Naomi and Larry's I do the do's. I *do*: light Shabbat candles, eat three meals, two with wine, have especially good food, preferably with guests. I *don't* understand, but who cares?"

"You don't just *feel* Shabbat, Mona?"

"I *feel* like I'm going out and getting pampered."

Then came the week that Naomi and Larry went out of town. "Let's make our own Shabbat," said Audrey.

Well, why should they give it up?

Aside from Shabbat, Mona kept herself too busy to think.

As much as the Jewish people keep Shabbat...

Maybe. But Mona and Shabbat had a relationship. A distant relationship. She would not get so close that she would have to think about what G-d did and did not want.

G-d would not want *her!* She had done something horrible. *Horrible,* and nothing could change that!

But where was G-d then?

Why had He let her do it?

Why had He put her in a situation where *that* looked like the best thing to do?

He knew what was right! Why hadn't He put other thoughts in her head?!

Why did He allow the conception?

Why didn't He give that conception to an infertile couple who were actually *praying* to *have* children? Why didn't He listen to them instead of tormenting her?

G-d had many strikes against Him. Yes, Mona and Audrey were "keeping Shabbat," and yes, they even became vegetarian during the week so that they were close to "keeping kosher." So what? She did this because she wanted to. Not because G-d said to.

So Mona wrestled with G-d. She didn't understand Him, and she didn't understand herself. Why *was* she keeping Shabbat? Why was she feeling guilty when she didn't?

"Two souls," Naomi explained. "We have a G-dly soul, and an animal soul. And, as *Tanya,* the fundamental text of Chabad Chassidus, explains, each soul wants total control. The G-dly soul wants us to connect to G-d by doing mitzvahs. The animal soul wants us to relax, eat nice food, lean back and enjoy. Neither one is going to let up."

The solution?

Naomi smiled. "Get the animal soul on our side. Show it what a great time it will have learning Torah and doing mitzvahs!"

Mona had smiled, enjoying Naomi's luscious Shabbat table. Surrounded by Shabbat at Naomi's, she had no complaints.

By the time Mona got her MA and moved to Brooklyn, she was basically keeping everything. She had been through a few Yom Kippurs, which somewhat helped. G-d gives us free choice, which means we can choose incorrectly, but also G-d forgives. G-d even forgave people who had done more terrible things than she had done. She read and reread the Talmudic story of Ben Durdaya, a sinner accomplished in every sort of transgression, who achieved such thorough forgiveness that he was called, posthumously, "rabbi." She learned that "repentance" is not exactly a Jewish concept. Jews do not "repent." They "do *teshuva*," which means to "return."

They "return" to their essential good and G-dly selves.

To "do teshuvah" there are three simple steps.

1) *Admit the wrongful act (to self and G-d).*

Mona admitted the wrongful act. No problem there.

2) *Regret it. Ask G-d and anyone else wronged for forgiveness.*

She regretted absolutely. She asked G-d to forgive. According to the books, G-d would forgive her. Anyone else wronged? Cliff was probably grateful. She prayed that the soul that could have been born would forgive her, too.

3) *Resolve not to do it again.*

Of course she would never do *that* again. But she didn't feel absolved.

She hadn't, couldn't yet, forgive herself.

One day, Mona met Levana at the hospital. Levana. Almost ethereal, spiritual, totally devoted to her very unwell mother. Daily, she sat by her mother's side, held her hand, wiped her forehead, swabbed her mouth. On Tuesdays she took a break for her weekly "charge up." She was going to Sarah's.

She invited Mona to join her. "Gourmet food and gourmet thought," she lured.

Mona bit. And there, before she even sat down for a challah roll, she met Rivka the matchmaker, who was eager to help Mona find her destined one, her *"bashert."*

Mona understood that not "everyone" was interested in a woman who had a child.

"So what? Who needs everyone? One right one is enough! You're a beautiful woman, you keep a nice home, you're smart—and you have a profession!"

Rivka found a nice young man. From Pittsburgh. A math professor. A genius, Mona was told.

He spoke in a monotone. *How do his students manage?* Mona imagined being a student in his class. Monotone every day for a semester? *Monotone every day for life?*

Okay, so not that one. Rivka didn't give up—she had a lawyer from Queens.

He was divorced, animated. Lots to say about the quirks of New York law. That was the first date. The second date he took her to a symphony concert, where he exhibited his encyclopedic knowledge of classical music. The third date, at a Glatt Kosher Manhattan restaurant, Mona was convinced that he was among the world's top ten authorities on mushrooms and wine.

But he had yet to ask her anything about herself. Not a team player, he. And wasn't marriage, especially the Jewish marriages she had seen, supposed to be a team effort?

She declined a fourth date. Declining was easy. She just had to say, "He's not for me."

In the years that followed, Mona did not find anyone who was right for her.

She didn't feel right for anyone, either.

* * *

Take Mona, take! Have something sweet for when you're home

Mona directed her consciousness back to Sarah's table. Sarah still had not come, and Tamar was summing things up. The luncheon was officially over, and an abundance of dessert remained on the table. "Take some for the road," encouraged Helen.

As Mona wrapped up a sampling of treats, Sarah returned from the Ohel, invigorated and feeling hopeful. Surely her prayers for Sholom would be quickly answered. Sarah greeted the remaining women, but went as soon as she could to the side room, eager to connect with Leah. She could almost hear Leah telling her that Sholom was fine, that the whole nightmare was already resolved. She reached for the phone...

"Sarah, please can I speak with you for a few minutes? I know you're busy..."

"Mona...?"

Yes, it was Mona, Mona wanting to speak with her, now. Sarah replaced the phone on the receiver. Mona didn't easily reach out... *a few minutes...*

Sarah refocused. Of course she had a few minutes. She'd make minutes. Sarah poured two cups of tea, set them on the kitchen table, invited Mona to join her.

"I've got questions I would really like to ask you," Mona finally allowed herself to say.

"Sure."

"I guess it really has to do with feelings."

"It can be rough out there."

"Yes! You have no idea how rough. As a social worker, I counsel others, and maybe if it were someone else talking to me, I would know what to say! But how do I…"

And she told all. Sarah wasn't judging. Sarah was listening. Wasn't Sarah there every day to help others overcome things like this that plagued them?

Sarah nodded as Mona spoke. A painful story, reflecting the anguish of a woman who had been in a difficult situation, with limited options.

"There is certainly no way out of this," Mona concluded.

"There is absolutely a way," said Sarah. "I can understand the guilt you feel, but that is all part of the t'shuvah process. T'shuvah means that we are "returning" to a relationship with G-d that is closer, stronger, more powerful than it was before. G-d wants it. He wants us to be very close. He gave us the gift of t'shuva because He doesn't want anything to come between us and Him.

"You know, if you have a falling out with someone you love, and you realize what caused it, and you resolve it, then through that falling out you learn about yourself and about the one you love. You can be more on the same page now, with a stronger and deeper relationship. That's what G-d hopes from us — the epitome of a loving relationship which we constantly strengthen and deepen. He even commanded us to love Him. *V'ahavta es Hashem. You shall love G-d, your G-d.* Our G-d. He's telling us that He is ours. When you love someone, don't you call them 'mine'?

"Every time we become closer to G-d, we get new tools to become closer still. When we catch our mistakes, we go from a negative to a positive. We also do t'shuvah by going from a positive state to an even more positive state. By learning Torah, doing mitzvoth, and increasing, our faith in G-d, we rise to an even higher, closer, level in our relationship with G-d."

Mona was not convinced. "Like how?"

"In your case, you have a deep understanding, which will enable you to help others in ways that few can. You can reach out to young women, and warn them of the psychological, emotional and physical effects of abortion that are so easily swept under the rug, where they evolve into one's personal monster. As a social worker, you have the tools and perspective to guide them. You could save lives.

"There's another situation, more subtle, where you could also be of great help. In large families, unfortunately, a mother can lose sight of her blessings through the diapers! A mother with many small children might feel isolated, overwhelmed, stressed. She might compare herself to other women who are getting a good night's sleep, who wake up refreshed, who have time to dress nicely, put on makeup, and go to work! That sounds pretty good to a mother who spends her nights staying up nursing a colicky baby. When she gets the news that she's expecting another blessing this mother needs encouragement. If someone like you would tell her how you admire her for raising this beautiful, thriving family, she would feel greatly encouraged. You might tell her that you have wished you could have had more children. And if you meet a woman who is expecting again, and feels it's too much for her, you can talk to her, find help for her, until she too sees that each child is a blessing. Maybe even tell her your story.

"And that is the essence of t'shuvah. Had your life not happened as it did, you would not be able to help those you can now, and save the lives that you can save now. It's your personal geulah [redemption]—breaking through old barriers, regretting an unfortunate negative, turning it over entirely, until it becomes a positive force that constantly deepens your relationship with G-d. This is personal redemption – on a very high level indeed. Do you know your Hebrew name?"

"Miriam."

"Miriam, Moses' sister, was a midwife, who assisted her mother, Yocheved. They were the chief midwives in Egypt. Pharaoh commanded them to kill every Jewish boy as the mother gave birth to him. At the risk of their lives, they refused to obey, and they saved a generation of children. You are certainly well named. May the power of your namesake give you strength."

Mona encoded this conversation in her memory, entered the concepts into her being until each word unblocked a troubled pathway to her heart and through her mind. She began to encounter opportunities to speak with women, helping mothers to enjoy their families, helping them find services, even helping the unborn to be born. Was this what she was created to do? She was feeling lighter, even relaxed, even grateful. Even worthy of blessings. And one mitzvah leads to another. Her journals took a different tone...

Women,

singing at the sea
Miriam leading
tambourine faith
Long before birth
the incubating soul
senses freedom
chooses life...
Chooses life!

Chapter Four
LEAH
NOVEMBER IN POSTVILLE

LEAH'S MORNING MEDITATION:

Modeh Ani l'fonecha...
I give thanks, before You, Living and Eternal King,

I give thanks to You, G-d, first thing when I open my eyes each morning, and I am used to really meaning it, because the first thing I'm used to seeing is my husband, who I love even more than on my wedding day over twenty-five years ago—love him differently, but love him more, and every morning I see him, there he is and isn't that a good reason to start the day with thanks? And suppose he isn't there? Then I'm not thankful?

For returning my soul to me,

Just being alive is reason enough to be thankful. Just being alive and being able to connect with G-d and do what G-d wants, because G-d does want, wants to relate to us and wants us to relate to Him, whatever situation He puts us in. He always knows the best situation to bring out the very best and deepest in us.

Mercifully.

G-d is merciful. It's good to think of that first thing in the morning, because in the groggy first moments of awaking, when what seems is so different from what is, that's when we most need to remember that G-d really *is* merciful. To have my husband in jail does not seem merciful. Yet Sholom, when *he* wakes up, he says *Modeh Ani*, including the word "mercifully."

Only very exceptional people can say "mercifully" and mean it when they are in prison. "Mercifully" in prison is different. "Mercifully" in prison means that for those few minutes that you are let out of your prison cell, no one else is using the prison phone, and you are allowed to make a call home. "Mercifully" in prison means that you have a chair to sit on and a light to learn by. "Mercifully" means that some moment during the day, you might be blessed to see the sun. In prison, Sholom says, one can become acutely aware of G-d's mercy.

He always has something surprising to say. In the most difficult circumstances, he makes me smile!

How great is your faithfulness!
Again, when I open my eyes in the morning, when my head isn't clear, when I look for my husband, and then remember he's not here, and why he's not, then my first clarified thought might not be how great G-d's faithfulness is.

But the text of the prayer does not change with circumstances. On days that are beautiful and good we don't alter the words and say how *extraordinarily great* G-d's faithfulness is. And on days that are difficult, and anything but the way that one wishes them to be, one does not say, Your faithfulness could be better today, G-d. G-d's faithfulness is great every day—just some days we have to stretch our mind to see it. Stretching the mind strengthens it. Or we can put our thoughts above the mind: have trust! Trusting in G-d makes things happen, Sholom says. G-d never deserts us. He is always with us. Okay, we have to have faith, sometimes, to truly believe that G-d is faithful. His tests are really tests of faith. Only the strong get tested. It lifts them to the next level.

I learned this as a child and Sholom learned this as a child. And how well did we really learn? Only a test would show if the learning penetrated the brain until it was absorbed into the heart. Sholom doesn't doubt. He has trust and faith that G-d does all for the best...

* * *

"Thank G-d!"

That evening Leah sank into the sofa, steaming tea mug in hand. She was ready to face the ominous stillness that had settled over Postville, and think.

Was anything still normal? Well, yes. Although her husband was in prison and although Postville was in chaos, the lives of her loved ones had not been totally overturned—the children still had a school to go to. They accepted what she told them, that they should pray for their father, that G-d does everything for the best, and that G-d would send him home soon. Of course, surely He would. Soon all would see how unjustly he had been imprisoned. Her husband was a man of integrity; he had real and dear friends who would surely rally behind him now!

She encircled the mug with her hands, felt the warmth, sipped slowly. How things could change overnight. She was a home-centered person—her focus was always on her husband and children. She was always there, for Sholom, with Sholom, behind Sholom. A new experience, being alone. An unexpected experience, being alone and spotlighted by menacing national media.

Such charges! Everything from illegal workers to illegal drugs. They even accused Agri of nurturing a meth lab.

The workers had been terrified. Mothers left without husbands, children without fathers! Leah now could relate to that all too well. After the raid, Sholom hired an expert international lawyer to help the workers through the legal labyrinth.

The workers were grateful until the second day, when the lawyer was told that he represented a "conflicting interest." In other words, as Sholom later discovered, the government was offering Agri's workers "u-visas" —essentially permanent residency in the United States—in return for testifying against her husband—

If the plant closed, Postville would lose its main source of revenue. Some said that the town would apply for public assistance as a disaster zone.

The impact was reaching beyond Postville.

For example, Mr. Rubin, earned a modest living from his small Brooklyn fruit store. The Friday after the Postville raid, Mr. Rubin kept his shop open as late as he could. He was waiting, hoping, for the gentleman who always came Friday afternoons, and bought up his remaining fruits and vegetables. For Rubin, this made the difference between making a go of his business and operating in the red. But that gentleman, a secret agent of Sholom Rubashkin, no longer had funds to buy up the leftovers.

Another example was Mr. Lander, who operated a men's shirt store. Lander would also have to close shop. Like Rubin, his margin of profit was just enough to pay his rent and feed his family. He had nothing left to restock his merchandise. Rubashkin had always supplied the shirts that Lander sold.

The far-reaching effects of Rubashkin's imprisonment would never be known.

Even to Leah.

Leah was trying to make sense of her situation. She had to focus on legal technicalities, strategies, agendas, making decisions, choosing counsel. Her world view was changing. She was a good citizen, the daughter of good citizens. She had never thought to question the justice system. But she had questions now.

Why had they stormed the plant to begin with? Why had they imprisoned her husband? Why did they demand a million dollars bail!?

She took a few sips of tea, not as hot now.

Ultimately, of course, she was in this situation for only one reason.

She was here because this was where G-d wanted her to be.

As she contemplated her life before, and her life now, all was essentially the same. All came from G-d, the same G-d that she prayed to every day. G-d had an amazing storehouse of situations. And everything, no matter how it appears at first, is ultimately good. Because everything comes from the Almighty, and from Him comes only good. Everything is for our benefit, no matter how it looks at the time. So she had always been taught.

Now she was being tested: How well had she learned!

People who couldn't imagine how *they* would react in this situation, were asking her how she was "coping" so well.

How?

You're not on anti-depressants? You're not taking tranquilizers? No sleeping pills? Not smoking? Not yelling at the kids? Not even bingeing on chocolate?

Everyone had their own coping systems. Many thought that if she didn't have a system similar to theirs, she had simply removed herself from reality. She was dreaming and in la-la land.

She wasn't dreaming. She was not in La-la Land. But she had stepped into a different reality.

When Sholom first heard rumblings that there could be a raid "somewhere within the hundred mile radius of the plant," he gathered the entire family to learn the *Duties of the Heart*. This classic work teaches how to strengthen our faith and trust in the Almighty. Sholom instructed his family, until they internalized that the Almighty, the Creator and Life Force of the world, does everything for our best, even when we can't see it. This understanding, this faith, was to be their protection, giving them strength physically, emotionally, no matter what happened.

So, yes, she did have a sort of system. She didn't feel that she had to "cope" as long as she could feel that G-d was right there with them.

And He was. He was winking at them, playing hide and seek with them, with them always, giving hints. True, they had to visit some unlikely places—places they never expected to step foot in.

She and Sholom inspired each other. They had a secret code.

Not that it had to be secret. She would gladly share. Their code was simply the first three letters of the Hebrew alphabet. *Aleph, Beit, Gimmel*. These letters stood for *Emunah, Bitachon, and Geulah*. Translation: Faith, and trust—bring the redemption!

She and her husband were hoping that these tests, the tests that they were going through now, would be the very last difficulty, for everyone, before the sudden arrival of Moshiach...

* * *

Roza Hinda, Leah and Sholom's oldest daughter, was certain that her father would be home soon. He *had* to be home soon. She couldn't see how her mother and her younger siblings could manage without him.

Yes, her mother was amazing. She never appeared flustered. She always looked lovely and put-together—make-up, tasteful clothing, coordinating shoulder bag. Always a smile, confident, in control, even relaxed and determined. *Aleph, Beit, Gimmel.* Her father's freedom, and the redemption of the whole Jewish nation—in the eyes of her mother, it was becoming more and more the same thing. Her father's imprisonment represented the Jewish nation imprisoned, exiled, among the nations. With his release, we will all be released, with Moshiach...

How much longer?

Unbelievable. Her father in prison? Her father needing a *million* dollars for bail and court expenses? Yes, exactly! But why be staggered by numbers! G-d provides everything. A million? Several million? Nothing is too much for G-d.

Her father, her grandparents, the whole family, had always been among the givers. Her grandmother established, and still worked in, her "restaurant" where the needy were treated like any other customer, yet received no bill. The whole family was like that. Not only to give, but to give with generosity, sensitivity, dignity. She grew up like that. The one who receives must feel that he is doing *you* the favor by taking!

As a young child, she hadn't caught on. In the evenings, she saw visitors come to her father's office. Important people. Her parents treated them with deference. They must have been dignitaries.

As she grew older, she came to understand that most of her father's visitors were actually needy. Some came for personal reasons—a child was not well, or they needed funds to make a wedding. Others represented organizations—a Chabad House, an orphanage, a yeshiva. And sometimes even their non-Jewish neighbors would come, like the farmer, Mr. Miller, who needed seed money for next year's crop. Didn't matter who you were, where you lived, where you prayed. What mattered, her father said, was that a person needed help.

Her father would smile and confide in her. "You *think* you are helping another. No. They are helping you more. Each one we 'help' is really giving us the mitzvah, bringing us blessings."

Even now, Roza Hinda didn't question the blessings. All G-d does is for the best!. Her parents trusted that there was good and looked for that good and found it, whatever happened. Whatever happened reinforced their ever-present faith in G-d.

It's all a test. Of course it's a test! Tests are designed to help us realize our strengths and belief. G-d does not give tests we can't pass!

All that she had learned from her parents resonated with Roza Hinda now. Now she was an adult, a young married woman. She and her husband had three young children.

To her husband she said, "We are going to raise a million dollars."

Her husband replied that he had a friend who had a list of philanthropists who lived in Monsey, New York. With a copy of that list, and with their three little ones in the back seat, they drove to Monsey. Her husband stayed with the children. Roza Hinda approached the homes.

What was she supposed to say?

Her mind wordless, she knocked on doors.

Sometimes a small child answered, just as she herself had answered the door when she was a little girl. Inviting in the "important people."

She had never imagined that she would be on the other side of that door.

People were kind. They wrote checks. For one hundred dollars. For one hundred and eighty dollars. For fifty-two dollars. She was well down the list, and had not yet collected a thousand! Her eyes burned. This was not working. They had to raise a *million!*

As her husband drove to the next address, she was afraid her voice would crack at the first word. She forced herself out of the car, stifled her feelings, rang another door bell. She pushed out the words. "Is your father in?"

He was. She met husband and wife. She accepted tea and cookies. The home looked so much like her parents' home in Postville. Warm. Comfortable. Mother, father, children. A library of holy books. A glass breakfront holding silver Shabbat candlesticks. Husband and wife sat down together with her, waiting to hear her story.

She explained the situation. They knew of her father, of the situation, what newspaper didn't comment on it. She mentioned the onslaught of Agri, and was about to describe the cruel treatment that her father had received in prison, unreasonable accusations, the myriad of charges designed to prejudice public opinion and jury.

The family was giving her their full attention, with kind eyes, just like her mother and father would have done...

She couldn't any more. She began sobbing.

"You want to raise..." the husband filled in for her.

"A million." She swallowed, composed herself. "So far I have seven hundred and eighty-six dollars. How can I..." She paused, to collect herself again.

"You've got the right idea," the husband said. "But the wrong numbers. This is the mitzvah of *Freeing the Unjustly Convicted Prisoner*, after all. Your father is being held captive, and we, the Jewish people, all have an obligation to free him. All you need is ten people who will give you $100,000 each."

All?

"I'll be the first. And I will help you find the others."

In that way, thanks to Divine Providence, Roza Hinda collected a million dollars.

She didn't yet dream that they would need millions more.

* * *

Postville News:

Sholom Rubashkin, Behind Bars, Bail Denied

* * *

"Sarah, they're not letting him out!"

Sarah, on the phone with Leah, didn't believe it.

"But—we raised the bail!"

"Yes—and we offered over eight million in collateral. Forty-three families offered to put up their homes—three shuls pledged their Torah scrolls—doesn't that show that he's trustworthy? But all the money in the world won't get him out. The judge ruled he's a flight risk."

"A what?"

"The judge claims he's a flight risk. Because he could fly to Israel, and claim dual citizenship. Because he's a Jew."

"So every Jew would be a flight risk?"

"Could be the court is setting a new precedent. No bail for Jews."

* * *

How could lasagna bake normally in the oven while her brother sat in prison? How does the world just go on! Sarah sat down, fuming. Corruption right here in America! Cozy America! Lifestyle doesn't get much better than this, until one's brother is denied bail. The prosecution added bank fraud to the accusation. And as the media pointed their scorching finger at her brother, people who should have known better gulped it down! People believe everything they read? Yet few went out to get the facts. If the community would only know, everyone would rally behind Sholom!

"Sarah!" Ora arrived unusually early. "How is Sholom handling it?" She didn't ask how *Sarah* was handling it. Sarah looked calm.

"*Your face is public!*" *Sarah's father had taught the clan. A face must not reflect anguish of heart. Thoughts are to be positive, and if one's heart fluttered, one's face must not show it.*

Ora embraced Sarah, noted that lunch was prepared, and yes, really, Sarah showed no signs of distress. Yet the jail with no bail was the final blow of a government raid that put Sarah's family's entire business on the verge of collapse.

"We're being tested," Sarah responded. "We don't understand why, but we trust that in the end Sholom will be vindicated, please G-d. *Think good and it will be good.* More than positive thinking, our thoughts can make happiness happen."

"*I read the papers. I* know what's going on!" Davida burst in and exploded. "Where's justice! He's the scapegoat! It's not an attack on Agriprocessors. It's an attack on *ritual slaughter*—an attack on keeping kosher!"

As Tamar, Helen, Joan, and Reva walked in, Davida raised her voice to include her new audience. "He's not the first Jew to be jailed, you know. Think of the Alter Rebbe and the Frierdiker Rebbe, arrested for spreading Judaism in Czarist Russia, and in communist Russia."

"Think of Mendel Bailas and the Dreyfus case," put in Reva, hooking her handbag to the back of her chair. "We're dealing with a kangaroo court."

"And everyone should know it," added Ora. "Talk about rotten press—it's totally slanted against Sholom. Thank G-d, Pinchus Lipshitz, publisher of the *YATED* newspaper, went to Postville, investigated, and got facts. He is supporting Sholom completely, even helping to raise money for the defense."

"PETA and the unions," Joan clicked her tongue and shook her head.

Reva nodded. Her husband, of blessed memory, had been a shochet, a ritual slaughterer, and she knew this topic. "They are clearly misinformed," she began. "Years ago, when we lived in Bangor, Maine, my husband worked as a shochet. The most humane way is in the Torah! We don't stun the animal first or shoot it between the eyes! Never! The animal should not even see the knife! And oh was that knife sharp — so sharp that the gullet and windpipe are severed instantly. The animal doesn't feel a thing! My husband was so careful. And he knew animal anatomy, just like a veterinarian, so he could check the organs of the animal to be sure it was kosher. I remember one entire shipment of lambs. Each one had pox on their lungs. Now if that pox could be removed, the lambs would have been 'kosher' but not 'glatt.' My husband tried, but could not remove it. Well, that didn't stop the FDA director. He came in and took the whole bunch. They were fine for the non-kosher market.

"I asked how anyone could eat them.

"'They just remove the diseased organ, and sell the flesh in the supermarkets,' my husband explained.

"And where did these laws come from?" Reva continued. "From the Creator, who created animals, and gave us His laws for slaughtering them. What could be more humane than that?"

"And what is Shalom doing there all day?" asked Helen. "The poor man is sitting all alone, wasting precious time."

"No, he doesn't waste time, even in prison," Sarah defended her brother. "You know, he cheers *us* up! He says he's able to daven and say tehillim. He's able to study Torah, even after all that happened to the plant. All he worked for—decades of toil and effort—well, we hope we can continue. Anyway, ladies, let's begin. We have a lot to cover today."

After the women said tehillim together, Sarah put herself in a different dimension and continued a previous discussion. "Our Hebrew name reflects our essence, and defines our mission in the world. The second of the five books of Moses, *Exodus*, is, as you know, called *Shemos* in Hebrew, and *Shemos* means names. G-d is calling to the essence of each of us."

"But names aren't specific. Look how many Leahs, Chanas, Yehudas there are!" said Tova.

"Right. But each name has a common thread," said Sarah. "For example, a chair. There are many kinds of chairs, folding, beach, dining room, desk, easy chair, overstuffed arm chair. Yet for all their differences, they have this in common: they are chairs! In the same way, all names are connected to the essence of the name itself. Every Sarah, every Rivka, every Rachel, Leah, and Chana, and so on, has certain traits that manifest differently in those who carry that name. Names give us strength, a sense of our purpose. We have names to be proud of."

"Our sages tell us that our life source comes channeled to us through our Hebrew names," said Ora. If a person faints, whispering her name in her ear can revive her."

"It does seem that people who have the same first name have certain traits in common," said Reva. "And we can check out the personalities of our ancestors. Our father Avraham was the epitome of kindness, and those who carry his name tend to be unusually kind as well. Yosefs are a little more than average concerned about their appearance. Rivkas are activists, hopefully for good—that's where you'll find them. A Sarah is a princess—with a sense of presence. And Devorah—means bee—I like their honey, not their sting!"

Tamar laughed. "Well, parents receive Divine inspiration so that the name they give their child will reflect the child's mission in life. And as Ora said, the letters of our Hebrew name, our name in the

Holy Language, form a channel through which we receive Divine energy. Our sages tell us that the letters of the Hebrew Alphabet are the vessels which the Creator used to create the world."

"My husband, of blessed memory, was also a *mohel*," continued Reva, "and he began to give out *Bris* certificates! Why? So that the Hebrew name would be in writing. Families often call their children by their English names. When the boy has his bar mitzvah, who knows if they will remember his Hebrew name!"

"What about a girl?" asked Aidel.

"True, no bris," said Sarah. "Girls are born perfect. We name them in shul, and have a kiddush. Now, regarding our Jewish names, I have a treat for us -- a letter that the Rebbe wrote about using our Jewish name." Sarah gave copies to the women, and Helen read.

From Letters from the Rebbe, Vol 4, Page 182, letter 114

Greeting and Blessings...I was particularly gratified to note that you have officially assumed your personal Hebrew names. This is certainly in keeping with the earliest Jewish tradition and something which was an important factor in the liberation of our ancestors from Egyptian bondage. For, as you surely know, one of the merits that brought about the Geulah [redemption] from Mitzrayim [Egypt} was the fact that the Jews there kept their Hebrew names and did not change them. And the significance of this is that a Hebrew name has a meaning and message that binds a Jew with G-d and His Torah and this is especially important when Jews are in Golus [Diaspora].

"Maybe I should start using mine," mused Helen.

A tall woman, a new face at Sarah's, had come with a purpose, and felt that now was the time to speak

"Sarah, my name is Devorah. I'm a social worker, and I've heard about your Tuesday learning group. I came here today, because I just can't sit still while your brother is in prison! Everyone knows of his philanthropic work and now he needs help! We've got to counteract the outrageous media coverage. We have to get out the truth! We have to get *him* out. We can't let the judge and jury decide his fate without showing them that the community cares! After learning today, let's let the ball rolling!"

When the learning session was over, women gathered round, and Devorah revealed her plan.

"This has to be really big," she began. "Judge Reade doesn't dream anyone will oppose her. She's about to discover the power of us woman! No way will we let Sholom remain unjustly in prison! We need to rally—let the world know, and raise money for Sholom's defense! We're fighting the U.S. Feds—we need big lawyers who cost big money. We've got to rally and raise it. I know that Beth El Synagogue will let us use their sanctuary. With balconies, it holds over two thousand people. I'll call Rabbi Snow."

"We need fliers and posters," said Yehudis. "I'll ask Uri."

"We need buses," said Tamar, "from Brooklyn, Manhattan and beyond. I'll make the calls."

"I can ask Pinchas Lipchitz, from the YATED, if he could speak about what he saw in Postville," said Ora.

Sarah nodded. "He could tell the real story and bring us up to date as to what's happening now."

"I wish Leah could be here," added Faygy.

"I'm sure she'll come if she can. Otherwise, let's videotape her!" said Ora. "We can show it at the rally."

"We should have some of the legal team speak," said Mona.

"I'll make announcements online," said Shaina.

"Miryam Swerdlov is a great speaker. I'll call her to be the MC," Reva volunteered.

Tzerl was chosen to lead the opening psalms.

"I'll do whatever else needs doing," Aidel volunteered. "Just let me know."

"Let's teleconference together tomorrow night," said Devorah. "We don't have time for more meetings."

Five days with sleepless nights flew by and the rally was born. Thousands came, from Brooklyn, Manhattan, Long Island, Monsey; bus after bus, woman pouring in with open hearts and open checkbooks. The sanctuary was packed to the third balcony, an awesome turnout. Leah, on video from her living room in Postville, addressed the women:

"We thank you with all of our hearts. We appreciate everyone's prayers and support. We rely on it. I can tell you now that I have no hesitation in going everywhere I can to get this story, this travesty of justice, out. This is an outrageous case for all Jews, not just Sholom. The bank was always happy to lend us money, and Sholom always paid it back. And now over 900 counts of fraud! And as Americans, we have to realize that it's also about every American. We are supposed to have laws of justice and we are supposed to have checks and balances. Where there are not, we have to show the government: this is not justice!

"We also have to spread the word. We have to use every venue, including our website: JusticeForSholom.com. We have to let people know what is going on. We have to show that justice is not being done."

The rally set off a chain reaction.

"Leah is just like Avital Sharansky!" enthused Reva. "I remember when Avital spoke at Yale. She travelled the globe, turned the world upside down to set her man free. Her husband was imprisoned in the gulag. Avital made endless petitions—and she got him out!"

"Our rally had reactions as far as Johannesburg," observed Shaina.

"Johannesburg hardly helps," said Davida. "Los Angeles, Chicago, Houston, Detroit, Baltimore, Boston — the American public opinion is what we need. Americans need to speak out, to write, to call the justice department."

"That's an idea," mused Devorah. "Let's contact respected lawmakers, former attorney generals, and law professors to speak out about this injustice. I read that another meat processor, accused of the same thing, got by with less than a year! They're talking about twenty-five years for Sholom? That's a life sentence!"

As the women began to organize the "contact respected people" idea, Yehudis suggested a Blessings Party. "Blessings bring blessings!" she said. "The more we bless, the more we become aware of G-d's bounty, and the more we open up channels for more blessings. I know how to put it together. Let's do it here next week."

The following week:

Not a normal Tuesday. Laden was the word. Fruit, vegetables, dips, cakes and crackers, and grape juice. Fragrant roses and lilies at the center of the table. Candies, chocolate, and sodas. Yehudis admired her handiwork, then addressed the women.

"We've always said blessings," she began, "before we eat, and after we eat, since we learned to talk. What is different here? It's the *amen* that is the big deal! Today we are all going to say blessings so that everyone else can answer amen!"

Tova nodded. "The power of amen. When you answer amen, you fuel the bracha! And you become a partner in the blessing."

"Have the right thoughts, too," said Yehudis. "When you hear someone saying a blessing before eating fruit, when you say amen, you should have in mind anything you need regarding children. Children are our fruit."

"If you want parnassah/livelihood," said Raizel, "have that in mind when you say amen to the blessing *mezonot*, like we say on cookies and cakes."

"Have your shidduchim needs in mind when you answer *amen* to the blessing for grape juice and wine," added Reva.

Sarah concluded: "Amen to the blessing *shehakol*, that G-d created everything by His word, is for all other needs. Ladies, when we answer amen to a blessing on the soda and candy, have Sholom in mind! We really need the blessings now... all that we can get..."

"Amen!" stated Rachelle.

Rachelle was delighted at the joyful, lavish table. She would just have to try a little bit of everything, such lovely fruits and pastries! For the blessings, of course! She would not overdo it, for she really was making a special effort these days to control her weight. Many women would like to lose five, or ten, or even twenty or thirty pounds. She, unfortunately, had to lose, well, a bit more than that! She certainly didn't want to gain back the few pounds she had worked so hard to lose, to qualify for that procedure...

Truly, these days she even had to be careful where she sat. A sturdy, stable, wide, solid chair was best for her. Yet, as she often told Sarah, she just didn't know where the weight came from. How much did she eat, after all? Didn't she control herself? And then she heard that only two extra cookies a day can tally up to hundreds of pounds over decades! Two little cookies! She had never realized that she needed *that* much self-control!

Really, what most excited her at Sarah's was not the food, but the learning. She gave a class in her own neighborhood, and she often quoted thoughts that she heard first at Sarah's. Yes, a good Torah class enlivens and enlightens one's conversation—and one's life. It's a pleasure to have some nice timely Torah ideas, to share with whomever you sit next to at a bris or bar mitzvah or wedding.

Rachelle came from a large family, she was blessed with a large family, and blessed also with many close neighbors and friends. How many happy occasions she shared, sometimes even more than one a night! How lovely, to rejoice in the happiness of dear ones, around a lovely table, with beautifully prepared food... Ah! Sarah was beginning the study part of the afternoon. Rachelle turned her attention to today's theme:

To leave our personal Egypt, the mind must rule the heart.
And nature is what habit makes it.
With our mind, we can control our thoughts, and reprogram our actions,
until the new program becomes our second nature.
We can, when we really want to...
Nothing stands in the way of will and determination!

Chapter Five
Rachelle

Several nights later...

Rachelle, sleepless, listened as her husband's words echoed in her mind.

"*Yes, Rachelle. We should save for retirement. And the first thing I want to save for our retirement—is you...*"

"Save... you... save... you..." Soul-felt words with as many facets as her wedding diamond, bold-faced a situation which she had hoped would self-delete. It did not. Rachelle had until six the next morning to decide: GO FORWARD with the procedure. Or: DO NOT.

Just now she was favoring the NOT.

NOT. A round, resilient word which resonated truth, determination, and backbone. Sarah would certainly not undergo such a procedure if it could be avoided. And shouldn't it be avoidable? Rochelle had just learned at Sarah's that the mind can and should rule the heart! Mind over matter! Reason above emotions! "*Are we robots, pre-programmed by desires?*" (Sarah had asked.) "*No! We are blessed with powerful brains!*"

Our powerful brains should certainly be able to curtail the appetite, and appease the stomach, Rachelle reasoned. Her own brain should be no exception. She should NOT need this procedure.

NOT. She eased her queen-sized body onto her back, stretched out her arms, her legs, luxuriating in the silky soft percale sheets that adorned her queen-sized bed. She filled her lungs with fresh air, slowly exhaling, inhaling again, exhaling. She relaxed. She was largely and beautifully comfortable. She basked in a favorite visualization: NOT to be banded.

Ah. Her stomach remains untouched, unrisked, unharmed by intrusions of any sort, no matter how "non-invasive." Her entire body, unsullied, happily basks in its glorious fullness, as it gently, naturally, reduces to the curvaceous adorable size twelve that she wore on her wedding day! Her wedding day...

Yes, her wedding day. The dawn of a new, sparkling era of her life. Surrounded by joyous parents, grandparents, family and friends, everyone near and dear, all so happy that she and her young husband, two halves on one eternal soul, had found each other and were setting off on their joyful life together. A life with a purpose and a goal: to build a beautiful family. They would be blessed, G-d willing, with good, healthy children who would love their fellows, love G-d, and keep and learn His Torah with joy and happiness. How everyone danced! And a five course meal!

She remembered planning the five courses. A fresh fruit cup, with strawberries, was to greet each guest as they entered the reception hall, as well as tehina, Israeli salad, and pickles. Does that sound passé now? How special it was then!

Next there was the hot, delicate mushroom pastry turnover and garden salad with chef's aromatic dressing. And the main dish—sumptuous roasted stuffed chicken, lovely whipped sweet potatoes, fresh green beans with slivered almonds, and a delightful little extra touch they had decided upon—a cranberry relish cup.

And finally, they served scrumptious Napoleons, with hot tea and coffee. How carefully she and her mother planned this menu. She remembered it to this day—although at the wedding itself, so busy was she with photos and dancing and greeting guests, she scarcely had time to taste anything! And she had been fasting the whole day!

Yes, the custom is that bride and groom fast on the day of their wedding, until the ceremony. The day of marriage is a private Yom Kippur for the bride and groom, a day of atonement and forgiveness, so that they may begin a fresh, new, life together...

Of course, they were not expected to enter the wedding hall starving. After the outdoor ceremony and blessings, but before they entered the wedding hall itself, she and her new husband were taken to the private room where they would be to be alone together for the first time. There he gave her a beautiful necklace, and there they were to eat a little meal. She remembered sponge cake, ginger ale, and special Golden Soup. Golden Soup for a golden life together—her aunt had prepared it, had it waiting for them, nestled under a bouquet of flowers, hot in a thermos. She remembered that Golden Soup. On the other hand, the five course meal, the dancing, the so many people who came to wish them mazel tov—this was all a blur, and would have remained so, had not the kind photographer preserved so many delightful moments in the wedding album. Her treasured white and silver wedding album, well worn over the years as children—and now grandchildren—looked through it, marveling at Mommy and Tatty (Bubby and Zaidy) on their wedding day.

So many blessings, G-d was so good to them, baby following baby, joyous occasion after joyous occasion, menu after menu. How many children? Children are not counted! All are healthy, thank G-d! That's what matters! The only little problem was that with each child she had gone up a size or so. One beautiful family after her size twelve wedding dress... she was, frankly, beyond size.

Why did she gain so much weight? Did she eat more than others, who seemed to gain no weight at all? Perhaps it was mazel—just her luck!

"Within a year," the band people said. "Within a year you could become a 12 again. From zaftig to svelte. The procedure almost guarantees it."

Oh, she would like that! Rachelle sighed, stretched her neck. She would have liked to fluff up her pillow a bit, but to move her arms so much above her head, that was an effort. She flexed her fingers instead.

Svelte! And wouldn't her husband like that! Of course, even now he thought she was beautiful. She always carried her weight well. A nice scarf at the neck, in becoming colors, a lovely *sheitel* (wig), a little well-placed make-up—she was, she always felt she was, an attractive woman. Attractive to her husband, as a woman should be. But svelte again! Why not! As she was in her youth, on her wedding day! Wouldn't that be wonderful!

Of course, they were and always had been a happy couple. Their lovely life and many blessings were shadowed only by the *Accurate to 360 Pounds Scale* which lurked in her bathroom. Usually she ignored it. And when she did use it, she could diffuse the punishment. Weight was relative! Her scale registered a perfect weight—for a large-boned, muscular male, about nine feet tall.

"I'm not overweight. I'm just short and the wrong gender!" she announced to Dr. Shiff.

He eyed her through perfectly polished lenses. "On the contrary. You are an excellent weight for three of you." He notated her chart; his meticulous handwriting left no room for error. "Unfortunately, you are only one, and that one is ripe for coronary failure, diabetes, knee and hip replacements, hypoglycemia..." He had his list.

"So I'll diet again!" She sighed.

He perused her record. "My investments should be like your diets—they always end in net gains."

She smiled brightly. "My appetite is recession-proof."

Schiff countered, with no smile. "I've done it, so can you."

The doctor stood up, his white, starched lab coat buttoned and belted. He was in shape. "Lost sixty pounds this year, Rachelle. Gave up smoking, too. Did it for my grandchildren, and G-d willing, my great-grandchildren. Not easy, but we're talking about life! I'm twenty years your senior, Rachelle, but I'm in shape. For you, there's no excuse. My prescription for you is serious lifestyle changes. Exercise! Moderate, healthy nutritional choices! There's more to life than food!"

Well, of course there was. She remembered this conversation as, still sleepless, she stared at her bedroom walls where tiny bits of light from the street lamp flickered through the curtains. It would be nice to turn on her left side, although side-sleeping was not so comfortable. Truthfully, her body wasn't as comfortable to be in as it once was. It had become, well, a little jello-y. Not her fingers and toes, not her hands and forehead, of course, but there was an abundance of jello-y-ness about the rest of her. It seemed to come on with age.

Dr. Schiff was insisting it came on with food.

She didn't see how. She hardly ate, she never binged. She did not overeat to the point of discomfort, no matter how tasty the food. She did not *crave* food. She simply ate three nice delicious meals a day, exactly what she prepared for her husband and children. Of course she enjoyed a few well-chosen snacks. The exceptional delicacies she saved for Shabbat. Everyone knows that you can't gain weight on Shabbat.

She should not be gaining weight. Of course, after every child she did expect to gain a little. Who didn't? Yes, a little gain after every child, a little gain which was not lost because another child, thank G-d, would soon follow. Eight little gains, but this was not so noticeable when one wore loose clothing. She had some beautiful outfits, outfits especially designed for the larger woman. Big and beautiful! Why not?

She was good with portion control. Her breakfast, lunch, dinner, and snacks were all reasonably portioned.

Lifestyle changes? What lifestyle changes could she make? What relationship with food should she alter?

Food was important! No one could live without it!

Rachelle wondered if Dr. Schiff really understood the relationship between life and food.

Sarah had spoken about it, and made an astute comment about Jewish life and food.

"Events in Jewish life are certainly made memorable by edibles," Sarah had said. "More than that, the foods are totally intertwined with the mitzvahs we do. A double catering service is what we need—to serve up mitzvahs to nourish the soul, as well as foods to please and nourish the body. Our soul not only resides in the body, but wants to team up with it. So we find interesting overlaps between the mitzvahs and the food du jour. Matzahs on Passover, honey on Rosh Hashanah, latkes-potato pancakes on Chanukah, hamentashen on Purim, Shavuot cheesecake. Even those who forget exactly what the holidays are about, remember the food..."

Yes, the relationship between serving G-d and serving a meal was complex and beautiful. As Sarah had explained another time, the body longs for physical food—and our soul does too! According to Kabbalah, our soul senses a spiritual spark in the food, and longs to elevate that spark. Part of each soul's mission is to elevate its particular quota of sparks. The soul passes this message on to the body, which says a blessing and then consumes the food. In this way the holy sparks are elevated.

How beautiful, Rachelle often thought, to be constantly elevating the physical, through food. To eat only for the pleasure of eating would be sheer gluttony, but the three Shabbat meals are mitzvahs, Yom Tov meals are mitzvahs and what about the meal at a bris? In fact, *any* food can be elevated. Just say a blessing before you eat, and a blessing after you eat, and use the energy of that food to do a mitzvah!

She enjoyed food—that proved that she had many sparks to elevate! Her soul had a hefty assignment! Yet she was determined to do her part. She discussed this concept with her husband.

And hadn't he agreed? "When food strengthens the body, it's a mitzvah to eat! Make a blessing before and after, and use the energy to please the Almighty!"

She liked what he said.

Then he added, "However, what is healthy for one person may be detrimental to another. We are forbidden to eat what is detrimental. So when we eat what is good for our health, it's a mitzvah. And when we don't eat what is detrimental to our health, that is a mitzvah as well!"

Rachelle sighed. Her husband explained things so nicely. Eat or don't eat.

Either way, a mitzvah.

But the truth of the matter was, thought Rachelle as she glanced at her alarm clock (not yet even one a.m.), the truth of the matter was she hardly ever *ate*. Some people *eat*. Pile a plate with food, finish to the last crumb—not a *refined* thing to do, and Rachelle never did. She used small plates, always, and took small amounts, always, and ate slowly, always. She had been certain that her weight gain must be hormonal. A medication, some small pill, could correct it! If her hormones would be balanced, she would not gain weight.

Dr. Schiff was not enthusiastic. However, he made the tests and called her with the results. Her hormones, he was pleased to report, were nicely balanced.

So she would need a different plan for losing weight. How many methods there were! At Sarah's, many of the women were fond of touting their own approach:

Davida: "I have the perfect product. One hundred percent kosher, and so delicious—and satisfying! The chocolate fudge flavor—totally yum! I lost thirteen pounds on it myself! You just mix one envelope with water, twice a day, instead of meals..."

Chana: "Exercise! Not necessarily do you have to eat less, just exercise more. And the rebounder is the best! Do it for twenty minutes—you've already wiped out half a piece of good chocolate cake!"

Yehudis: "There's nothing wrong with fasting. We do it five times a year and many could benefit by doing it even more. Everyone needs a vacation, including the liver and stomach and kidneys!"

Gitti: "Spend the money on *tzedaka* instead of food. I'm collecting today for my son's yeshiva. People who eat more than they should, should remember those who can't pay for what they need." She passed around an envelope for contributions.

Ora: "Affirmations! Amazing what you can do! Smile, look in the mirror, and say out loud: *Every day in every weigh I'm getting better and better!*"

Helen: "Self-discipline. Dieting takes tremendous self-discipline. You must change the way you habitually eat. But as I told my students: Once you break one bad habit, you'll have the strength to break them all."

Mona (in an undertone): "People who don't have a weight problem can't understand people with a weight problem. I hate my bathroom scale!

Faygy: "A lot of ladies these days are doing yoga."

Reva: "A balanced diet is key. I always have fruit for breakfast. It's light and satisfying. And a soup and sandwich for lunch, and broiled fish makes a good dinner."

Tova: "Do what Aidel does. Make up a whole platter of cake, and play hostess! Make sure everyone *else* gets a piece!"

Aidel: "It's true. Sharing with lots of friends is more fun and less calories."

Shaina: "Try celery. You burn more calories digesting it than you got from eating it."

Tamar: "Why do we have to spend so much time talking about food! Use the intellect! Learn! When our *mind* is on other things, we lose weight!"

But the conversation did not end there.

Lily: "Bread is life. In the camps we really understood the meaning of a crust of bread!"

Sarah (in silent thought): *Shalom had to go on a hunger fast before they would give him kosher food!*

Levana: "To thank G-d properly we do need to appreciate food, and see its beauty, and its wisdom. Did you know that when a palace fire burned the recipe books that contained half the known recipes for dates, Rabbi Yehuda HaLevi mourned! He said that this was a great loss, because every recipe brings out unique aspects of G-d's creation. Fully appreciating dates heightens our appreciation of the date's Creator!"

"Dates are a lovely food," Rachelle had readily agreed. "And half the recipes for dates were *not* lost. I wonder where those recipes are now…"

As a result of that discussion, Rachelle stopped off at an excellent fruit market on her way home. There she bought several pounds of their best dates, and enjoyed a good portion of them before dinner.

Rachelle concluded that these methods weren't for her. Who could understand? She loved food. The tastes, textures, aromas, the pleasing appearance, the thought that G-d in His love for humankind supplied these delights!

Hadn't she developed a deep love of G-d through her love of food?

She had, but she still needed to lose weight. And while everyone had well-meaning suggestions, these were suggestions for maintaining a chosen weight. Maintenance was not her issue. She needed serious reduction.

She decided to consult with friends who had succeeded in substantial weight loss. She called Tzippy.

Tzippy wasn't answering. She had recently married a semi-retired widower and their new life together apparently put less important matters on hold. Finally Rachelle pinned her down for a *tete-a-tete* breakfast. Rachelle ordered a lovely corn muffin with her coffee. Tzippy had half a melon.

"My diet calls for melon for breakfast," Tzippy volunteered. "Drink a glass of water with lemon juice as soon as you wake up. Two hours later, a half a melon. It could be honeydew or cantaloupe. Have watermelon once in a while.

"A half hour later you can have some tea. Lunch is protein, like broiled fish, but no carbs. The whole thing is about what goes together. Fruits are separate, proteins are separate. You can mix carbs and vegetables. I love the diet. You never get hungry. You can always eat something."

"Well, how do you stay on it?"

Tzippy smiled. "You know me. I never was one to keep to a diet. I was no skinny pickle when Abe died, may he rest in peace. And after that what did I care? Food was my comfort, my solace. But what happened was Abe's brother's best friend's neighbor is Al, who had lost his wife a little after Abe passed away. So everyone thought Al and I should get together. Well, I knew that Al was a very fine man. But after Abe passed away I gained thirty pounds. I'd need three of Al to make one of me! Had to work fast. So I dropped eight pounds before we met, and the world's tightest girdle, and lowest lighting, got me through our first date. I lost ten pounds while we were dating, and another fifteen between the engagement and the wedding.

"Al only says the nicest things to me—how he never thought he'd be happy again, and how beautiful I am, and how proud he is of me. I just melt—literally! Really, what's a cupcake next to a compliment? And, yes, I do have this little diet, and yes, I follow it, and yes, I can give you the name of the book. But for me? Al is my breakfast, lunch and dinner. G-d is so good to me. I am just crazy about Al. We have a very active life together. And I totally don't miss food!"

Tzippy had to leave to meet Al, while Rachelle lingered a while, sipped tea, and crumbled her corn muffin into flakey crumbs, which she savored as she contemplated the conversation...

Muffins. Rachelle clearly recalled that muffin, as she adjusted her body so she could eye the alarm clock on her nightstand. Twenty after one. Late nighters were circling the block looking for parking spaces. Many hours lay ahead of her, and she would be happy to savor another muffin. However, one was not allowed to eat after nine o'clock on the night before the procedure.

Tzippy's story had not been helpful. Rachelle's husband certainly inspired her, but it was not that breathless, new-love kind of inspiration. Ah yes. She remembered what that was. Before her wedding she had also dropped a size or two! And after that, she hadn't gained an ounce until her pregnancy. Imagine!

As it happened, soon after her meeting with Tzippy, she had that historic get together with Claire.

They ran into each other at the dry cleaners on Sixteenth Avenue. Rachelle couldn't believe it. Her childhood friend, with whom she used to share recess snacks, and who at last sighting was even heavier than Rachelle, had diminished to hardly a shadow of her former self. Rachelle immediately invited Claire to join her for coffee.

They stepped into one of Rachelle's favorite cafes. Claire ordered a cup of green tea. Nothing else. Rachelle, who had not had a proper breakfast that morning, noted that the cheese danishes were delightfully fresh and plump. However, she ordered only one of them. And she ordered a coffee, with her usual two creams, but no sugar. Yes, no sugar. She always made that sacrifice. A spoonful of sugar is 16 calories, two is 32 calories, and it does add up. Anyway, with a nice danish, one hardly misses sugar in coffee.

Claire slowly sipped tea, as Rachelle stirred her coffee and anticipated the danish. "Won't you have some?" she offered graciously.

Claire smiled. "Thanks, but no."

"You look so nice, Claire. Quite amazing. You know, I also have to lose weight. How did you do it?"

"Oh. Well, I really had to change my eating habits."

"But how?"

"Oh. Well, at first it's hard. Murder. Later isn't much easier. But if you can deny yourself once, then again, and finally again, which means, do it once, and then twice, and then three times, well by then you have a vested interest in succeeding. You think: If I give in now, then I'll have to do the beginning all over again, and the beginning is so hard. So you just persevere, until, eventually, a new habit becomes second nature..."

Nothing new there. "Did you have at least a support group?"

"Oh, you can always find a few women for an emergency pep talk..."

"Exercise?"

"Well, whatever, as long as you do it..."

"A diet plan?"

"Portion control is really..."

"Doctor?"

Claire pursed her lips. "Goldvurm on 5th Avenue. It's torture, but it's the only thing I could get to work. Don't tell anyone!"

"How can I tell? Whatever you said I've already forgotten!"

Goldvurm on 5th Avenue. Rachelle pondered what kind of masochistic diet Dr. Goldvurm advocated. She discussed it with her married daughter, Bella.

Bella laughed. "Ma—he's the band."

The band?

"Yes, big secret. People who can't close their mouths close their stomachs. It's surgery. Closes off most of the stomach. So little is left—two bites and you're full. Then people lose weight."

Oh.

The idea left Rachelle speechless. To mutilate the stomach because one could not control one's mouth? Hi-tech barbarism! Other solutions must exist!

But this solution seemed to work.

The idea hovered in her mind until she came across an article in a respectable Jewish family magazine. The article was written by a fine woman whom Rachelle knew personally. As she read, she began to wonder whether certain women, who had suddenly succeeded in losing great amounts of weight, might also have undergone this procedure! Secretly, of course. Well, banding was what you did when all else failed. And who wants to admit failure?

On the other hand, these who "failed" did succeed in losing weight.

They succeeded in all the benefits that come with weight loss: They succeeded in feeling good about themselves, in wearing clothes that were not shapeless, in pleasing their husbands. They succeeded in easily climbing stairs, in strengthening their hearts, in not being at risk for all the ailments that previously threatened them. They succeeded in not being half prisoners to their homes, total prisoners to their bodies.

They succeeded in saving their health, even their lives.

Success.

The article did, however, also mention a recuperation period, which did not sound comfortable, as well as a window of time when complications could occur. Follow-up operations could be necessary. Also, the body's skin might not be able to shrink down to the body's new size. Plastic surgeries might be required. Definitely a whole new set of risks.

The article also mentioned a small mortality rate.

Of course, the more experienced one's surgeon, the better the odds. It seemed that Goldvurm had lots of experience.

But the worst was yet to come: Some people gained back the weight! Imagine going through all of that and...

No mention was made of the cost of the operation. Well, if the operation was lifesaving, it would be worth any cost.

And if it were life threatening?

But if it worked!

If it worked, one would only be able to eat tiny amounts of food—forever, if one was stapled. With the band, it was actually adjustable. Before the holidays, or before a *simcha*, one could actually visit one's doctor, and have the band widened. One could then eat more! What a blessing to be able to control one's appetite!

But so extreme? Weren't there other ways? Like perhaps one could find a Kosher Diet and Exercise Camp, where one could exercise maximally, be fed minimally, and one could lose fifteen, twenty, even thirty pounds in a long summer.

And one could gain that weight back in a short winter.

Well, she would ask around, investigate. But she had a hunch—or was it a wish?—that this band thing might work for her.

* * *

There were many who thought it would work for them.

Rachelle began to notice many overweight individuals who suddenly found "a program" that worked, who had, in fact, been banded. In due time the topic arrived at Sarah's.

"They think they look beautiful. But their faces really looked better before."

"Are you kidding? Gaunt is the word. Positively starving!"

"They are starving. With redesigned stomachs two bites is the limit. How healthy is that?"

"Still healthier than being two hundred pounds overweight!"

"Must be other solutions."

"How 'bout banding the mouth?"

"They are addicted to food! Food is their love and comfort—food is their sabotage and enemy! Can't live with or without it."

"Extreme, but some need it. What's the choice if nothing else works?"

"You can make it not work."

"That's true. I know at least five people who banded, and gained back every ounce!"

"But not everyone does. The programs provide coaching, counseling..."

"What happened to *the mind rules the heart*?"

"The heart succumbs more easily than the stomach!"

Sarah didn't denigrate the band. "Everyone's different," she said. "Banding is a personal question. But if a weight issue is becoming a threat-to-life issue, the brain might decide that the best way to control the appetite is the band."

Had Rachelle tried everything else? *Had* nothing else worked? Rachelle again consulted her daughter Bella.

"Ma, you could go around the alphabet with all your diets!"

Rachelle, not yet sleeping, recalled her daughter listing the diets. If diets were like sheep, she would fall asleep counting them.

"The Acupuncture diet, the Buddy diet, the Chili Pepper Diet, the Diet of All Diets, Exercise and Diet, Fact and Fiction Diet, the Gelatin Diet...

She got to T. Not yet sleeping, Rachelle recalled diet details:

The Tender Diet—prepare attractive, really lovely meals for yourself, within your calorie allowance, and eat with friends.

The U-diet. U make up your own diet, just stick to it.

The Very Healthy Diet: only organic produce and whole grains.

The Watermelon Diet: great if you like watermelon.

The Xtra Lean Diet—follow this simple diet and exercise plan until you become extra lean.

The Why Diet? A guide to making lifestyle changes that will end forever your need to diet.

The Zylla Tribe Diet—Although most of the foods in this diet have yet to be exported, most non-Zyllas find that simply reading Zylla recipes will suppress the appetite...

And she had tried not only diets, but therapies, exercise, hypnosis, visualizations, even self-deception. (She was advised to imagine that delicious food was really a horrible, disgusting thing! What an outright lie!) Meanwhile, living as she did in a walk-up third floor condo, the walk up was becoming a steep climb. More and more it wasn't worth the effort to go out.

If she continued like this, she really would be a prisoner to her body.

Suddenly, as sleep began to descend heavily upon her, Rachelle envisioned her body in stark reality: massive, expanding, and indeed helpless. She needed a salvation. She would—she resolved that she would—go through with the procedure. She would do the band...

So she did. She did it, had it done, all in a blur, dream-like, of course. The procedure was over now, and she felt herself rising up from it, stiff, achy, nauseous, just as they had warned that she would be. Stiff, achy, nauseous, but svelte!

No, not svelte. Not at all svelte. Nothing changed! Every ounce of her was still there! She felt awful—an awful she had never felt before, so stiff, achy, nauseous—and hungry. Thirsty, too. She looked up, blinked. A woman was smiling down at her. One of the band support people, offering a thimble-sized drink with a straw the width of a hair. Rachelle sucked at the straw, emptied the glass. Barely enough to moisten her tongue!

She sank back into deep sleep, and woke up, groggy, in a different room. Here she was offered dinner: Two spoonsful of vanilla yogurt. One spoonful of cherry jello.

A joke?

"Don't worry," the band lady encouraged her. "In three short hours, you can eat again!"

Oh. Even half asleep, Rachelle recognized the band center's "positive portion" philosophy: the end of the meal is not to be understood as the beginning of deprivation, or worse, starvation. Understand that the meal's end is part of a continuum. The end of one meal will indeed continue with the beginning of another.

Eventually she graduated to a half inch cube of roasted chicken, two thimbles full of whipped potatoes, and three peas!

A sparrow would starve. How could she survive?

Days passed in a blur, but she was surviving. Deprived, but surviving. She had been warned of the dreadful consequences of overeating and dared not, no matter how desperate she felt. To eat so little in this land of plenty! Her only joy during those early days was employing her former enemy, the bathroom scale. Yes, indeed, the pounds were coming off. Her tent-type wardrobe was still serviceable for the first month, and for the second. But she was losing! After ten weeks she treated herself to a new outfit. Her size was still beyond size, but didn't she look thinner? She was getting used to miniscule portions. Ah, the sweet taste of success!

People began to notice. Rachelle, you look wonderful!

And she felt wonderful. She was really losing weight! An excellent support group gave her courage, guidance. When she graduated the support group, she became a counselor. She encouraged others!

Yes, she saw it all happen. She thrilled, she amazed herself. She, Rachelle, svelte in a darling size 12, counseled and supported other women who visited the center, in bodies three times too big. She listened to their stories. She encouraged them. And that encouraged her even more. She had succeeded. She was a success.

For a while. For a while she could barely eat two bites. Two bites and she *couldn't eat more!* And if she tried to eat more—just a little bit—well, she soon saw what a mistake that was. No food was worth that. She learned her capacity. She could exist on that.

And her loved ones were delighted. "Ma, you look fantastic!" Bella couldn't get over it. And her husband! He was always proud of her, always loved her, but didn't he stand taller now when they went out together, and didn't he care more now how *he* looked! He even bought a treadmill. Together they acquired a taste for healthful food, for what was called "quality eating." The few bites she did eat had to pack in nutrition, obviously.

Of course, as the overweight melted away, her stomach capacity did increase a little. That was normal. After all, once she reached her goal weight of one hundred and thirty-five pounds, a fine weight for a woman of her age, height and bone structure—even Dr. Schiff said so—well, with that goal achieved, she couldn't expect to *live* on just two mouthfuls. Even with nutritious foods, she needed to adjust to something that resembled a normal, although conscientious, of course, meal.

Thirty pounds slipped on in a blink.

"Get rid of it!" warned friends at the Program. "Now!" They all knew the horror stories—banded women who gained it back, all back, and more!

No! Where was her control? She lost a little, she gained more. Was she really back to where she started? Diet after painful diet, always with a net gain?

She'd soon be up to a size 18...

Now she really had tried everything. Could it be there was no solution?

Her Program said to keep a "food log." Write down every mouthful, they dictated to her, just as she had advised others. She had read many food logs.

Everyone had their own point of departure. Perfect until 6 p.m. And then! Or perfect until I go out to eat... or perfect until I pass the bakery... or perfect until there is a joyous occasion... perfect until I'm alone... Everyone had their level of perfection and point of departure.

She found that she herself had many points of departure. All very small, of course. After all, her stomach couldn't handle much. Her portions were measured, and controlled, but space permitting, she controlled on the generous side.

It seemed that space was increasingly permitting.

But she had limits. She only ate certain desserts at specified occasions as a treat. Occasionally, as a treat, she allowed two.

She was strict about snacks. Only occasionally did she permit snacks other than at snack time. Furthermore, after her evening snack, she did not allow further snacking. Occasionally, she did permit a late-evening snack.

When she added up the extras, when she finally did write down the unremitting log, she found that her point of departure occurred about 12 times a day, and that in general she more than doubled her allotted calorie intake.

Her light, her happiness was quickly dimming. She knew all the tricks, could teach them to others, yet she could not teach herself. She became a helpless bystander as she watched her body, expanding, expanding, expanding up all the sizes, 14, 16, 18, 20 W, 22W, 24W, extra, extra, extra large—as the stairs again winded her, as the jello-y-ness of her body returned with the familiar jiggledy-ness so appealing in jello molds, but for herself, rolling herself out of bed was taking greater and greater effort. Then her alarm clock rang at 6 a.m...

The alarm was ringing. Rachelle hoisted her arm up, clutched the clock, turned it off. Her arm was so heavy. She was so heavy. But banded? Had she been banded, or had she NOT?

NOT. She still had not, despite a most convincing dream to the contrary.

Still not!

However, by the end of the day, she could be.

Yes. In a few hours, she was to be lying on the operating table. She would be skillfully anesthetized, and then, in the least invasive way possible, she would be sliced, rerouted, and banded.

She could if she would.

Rachelle sighed deeply, and sank back into her queen-sized pillow.

She wouldn't.

She had decided. She would not.

* * *

"Ma! Ma!! You missed your appointment for the band! You were supposed to wake up and go for the procedure!"

"I couldn't. How could I do that to myself?"

"Ma, we talked..."

"Talk! One can talk to try something on, so to speak. Try on, and then try off."

Rachelle addressed her unconvinced daughter.

"You know me, Bella. I'm committed. Until now, my commitment was to eating. It's just logic. If I don't shift that commitment, even the band won't help."

At first, still under the impact of the Night Before the Procedure, Rachelle put herself on auto-pilot and found herself heading for the extremes: diet protein drinks for breakfast, lunch, dinner, and nothing more. By day she volunteered at a nearby nursing home, helping to feed the elderly their lunch. They were on soft diets. Mrs. Magdoles smiled and nodded as Rachelle took bland, pasty spoonsful of cream of rice, and offered them. No taste, and barely lukewarm. But Mrs. Magdoles ate and smiled. Couldn't talk, couldn't walk, could hardly move—could eat, and seemed grateful for the feeding. Others were less grateful, some downright displeased. Their diet was monotonous, unappetizing, and did not tempt Rachelle in the least. Yet cream of rice nourished, and was within the digestive capabilities of the recipients. Mrs. Magdoles was smiling. Mrs. Magdoles, some said, was more than one hundred and three years old.

Rachelle wrote Mrs. Magdoles' story in her journal.

"Alas! Today's impact may not affect tomorrow!" She knew herself well. She put locks on the fridge and the pantry. Her husband had the only key.

She lost five pounds the first week and did *not* think how much more she had to lose. Nor did she fantasize about the treat she would allow herself when she lost X number of pounds. She would delight in *each* pound lost. She added some inspiring stories to her journal.

This from Sarah's: Rabbi Levi Yitzchak of Berditchev wanted to show how a Jew serves G-d. He called his simple Jewish servant in, and asked him why he ate. "I eat to live," was the reply. "And why do you live?" "I live to serve my Creator."

Then he called in his Russian servant, Ivan. "Ivan, why do you eat?"

"I eat to live," replied Ivan.

"And why do you live?"

Ivan smiled. "I live to eat!"

The following week Rachelle decided to exchange the breakfast diet drink for a soft boiled egg, a glass of freshly juiced vegetables, and a finely cut green leafy salad, seasoned with lemon juice. She also walked downstairs every day, to get the mail. That week she reminded herself about the "religious" evil inclination, which would not dream of asking her to eat non-kosher food, but urges instead,

"Say a blessing! Eat! Eat!!"

Habits are hard to change. Yet nothing stands in the way of will and determination.

The following story Rachelle heard from Rabbi Yossi Jacobson:

In the 1940's smoking cigarettes was the social norm, and was not considered unhealthy. The previous Lubavitcher Rebbe, who was in delicate health, was a heavy smoker.

One day a doctor came to visit, to explain to him the hazards of smoking. The doctor made a strong case, with charts, facts, and figures. After he spoke, he took out a pack of cigarettes, and offered one to the previous Rebbe, who questioned this action.

"I am going to smoke," explained the doctor. "Since you are a smoker, it's only polite that I offer you a cigarette as well."

"You are mistaken," was the reply. "I was a smoker. I listened to what you said. I am not a smoker now."

Nothing can stand in the way of will and determination!

So Rachelle persevered.

* * *

Glimpses Behind Bars

As Providence would have it, one of Sholom's cellmates was Keith Williams, a former judge, raised Presbyterian. The deep friendship that they formed gave their challenging prison days both hope and meaning. Keith requested a copy of the *Gutnik Chumash* (Old Testament), which Sholom's sister Chayale sent to him.

When Sholom was transferred to a different prison, Keith continued to correspond with Chayale and her husband. Sarah shared excerpts of these letters with the women. This week Keith wrote: "*When Sholom tells you stories of how cold his cell was, it is no embellishment. I did not have a decent night's sleep because of the cold. Sholom was always reminding me that all things come from G-d, and He always sends good things, although sometimes the good is well hidden. I remember that lesson every day. Meeting and getting to know Sholom is certainly one of the good things from this place. I look forward to my family sitting down with the Rubashkin clan in comfortable chairs, someday.*"

Sarah's sister Rachel Leah called from Israel every night. "What's going on?' she had to know. "What's happening now?" One night Rachel Leah seemed to be sobbing, losing control. "Sarah! Sarah—what can we do! What is going to be with him?"

"Calm down, Rochel Leah," Sarah said. "You can look at it two ways, and you have a choice. You could be terrified. Or you could think positively, get a grip, hope, and keep doing uplifting things—and G-d will help us! Learn from Sholom! He's the one in jail. But he's not losing it. He's organizing his time, *davening*, learning. It's a test—we are all being tested. And we're pulling together, praying, doing good deeds, as well as putting the best lawyers on the case. So let's not put in any negative energy. You'll see, he'll be vindicated. We're sure he'll be home soon!"

"Look at the themes of Chanukah," Sarah greeted her guests, Tuesday of Chanukah. "Light over darkness, the few over the many, the season of triumph. It's time to lighten things up. We received a letter from Sholom, a letter that he sent from behind bars, to the family and close friends. I'd like to share it with you."

B"H

To my dearest family and friends,

Chanukah is tomorrow. On Shabbat Chanukah we read the Torah story of Joseph, who became Prime Minister of Egypt and saved the Egyptian people from famine.

Joseph brought blessing to Egypt; my father and our family brought blessing to Postville. With G-d's help my father invested his money, time, and family into an abandoned part of the country. Our business attracted other business to the area and Postville, Iowa, flourished. Everyone benefited.

But in time, the leaders in Postville forgot these blessings.

Why was a flourishing town left in ruins?

As I sat there in the big courtroom of justice, watching the libel continue, it dawned on me what a smelting furnace is.

How is it different from a melting pot?

America prides itself on being a melting pot. Many different people come here and assimilate. They lose their distinctive characteristics. They become Americans.

In Egypt, the Jews did not enter a melting pot. They entered a smelting pot. What a difference that letter "s" makes! The Jewish nation entered into a "smelting pot," where a difficult process takes place. A melting pot creates a single homogenous mass from a variety of distinct, separate ones. A smelting pot refines what enters it—separates the gold from the dross that was bound up with it.

I am going through a smelting furnace. The gold of my Jewish soul is being separated from the dross. After undergoing this I understand as never before *Ashrainu*. How happy we are, and how great is *our* portion. May G-d bless each of us and all of us with the coming of Moshiach!

A happy Chanukah!

Sholom Mordechai HaLevi

Rubashkin Cleared of State Charges

Davida was waving the headlines, hot off the internet—Sholom was cleared of charges for hiring under-aged workers.

The women gathered at Sarah's to celebrate. Mrs. Rubashkin kissed everyone, and thanked everyone for their help. She was ecstatic about the support her son had received since the rallies. Justice! Pursue Justice! She and her husband knew adversity—they had run from the Nazis, scrounged to stay alive. "When you have faith, G-d helps you! During the war we had faith and we survived. And we believe G-d will help Sholom!"

"When two Jews say l'chayim, wishing each other well, it triggers blessings from Heaven," Sarah said as she served plates of cake with tiny glasses of sweet liquor. "Let's make a l'chayim, that Sholom be free, and may G-d bless all of us in whatever we need." Sarah continued. "Sholom never expected to be the catalyst of such an outpouring of unity. You know, he's receiving 'fan mail.' Letters saying, 'Chin up!' 'Justice will prevail!' 'We're in your corner.' 'We pray for your release.'"

Mrs. Rubashkin added, "They even believe that Sholom is a tzadik [righteous person]—they ask that he should pray for them!"

The only remaining accusation was the federal charge, to be adjudicated by Judge Linda Reade.

Sarah smiled. "We need to be as happy as we can. Happiness breaks through barriers. When you trust so much in the Almighty's benevolence that you are happy no matter what, then He gives you something to be happy about…"

Chapter Six
REVA

REVA'S DIARY, WEEK AFTER MOSHE'S FUNERAL:

I know that where I am is where I have to be and how it has to be. I sense G-d's presence in my life, that He is watching me and taking care of me. It's what G-d chose for me, and it must be right for me. We are commanded to be b'simchah—happy—in every circumstance. I have free choice. I can choose to be happy.

Among Reva's memories of those first foggy days after Moshe left this world was of her husband's rented hospital bed being taken from their room.

Now her bedroom had only one bed.

Moshe...

She believed that G-d knows how long a person should live. She believed that when a person has finished their mission in this world, they pass on to the next. Moshe, clearly, had finished his mission. The "holy sparks" that *he* had to elevate had been elevated.

He was not in this world any more. That hurt.

Hurt hard, like a pain in her chest. Hard hurt, while her bed stared back at her.

Her bed. Alone, strange, unbalanced at one side of the room. A dwarfed, single bed.

She faced it, moved it, to the center of the room. She placed a small, soft rug nearby.

She was still here, and her mission was not yet over.

That first week, the week of *shivah*, was a daze. Moshe had been ailing for so long. There had been ups, they always emphasized the ups. But there had been downs. She never admitted it, yet she forced herself to be strong as the base line kept lowering. Dehydration, or bedsores, or bloating, or breathing, always a new crisis, yet she hoped and prayed for a miracle. Please, G-d, give us more time.

She knew he was fading.

That last hospitalization was the worst. They had the kindest of nurses, the angel nurse, who said, "Don't resuscitate. It's not going to get better."

Backed by her four children, Reva never gave that order.

At night, alone, she imagined what the final moment would be like. She imagined, as though to prepare herself, yet when it happened she was numb.

Ultimately, there's no preparation, although Jewish law gives structure that supports one during the ordeal. There was the *shivah*, the seven days of mourning, when she grieved, but not alone. The stream of consolers helped blunt the initial pain. And then there was *shloshim*, the first month. She continued to grieve, but every day a touch less. Her children would mourn for a year. A year for a parent, for one has only one mother and one father, and they cannot be replaced. But for a spouse? Jewish law allows the living spouse seven days of grief, followed by three weeks of intense mourning. One mourns only for one month. The law forbids over-mourning.

After that first month, her children constantly called her, visited, checked up on her. And her friends. Her friends called, always some excuse for calling, to see how she was. Usually their calls were a comfort.

Not always.

"Oh, hello, Baila."

"Reva! Oy, Reva, how are you? I'm so sorry! It's so hard—and it doesn't get easier! I'm still missing my Jerry after eight years!"

"Oh!"

"Yes! We had our thirty-third anniversary—and then he passed away! And I used to do everything for him—cooking, cleaning, helping with the business—he was my life!"

"I'm sure he was."

"And our Elaine and Larry, of course. Now Elaine's in Nevada with Joel and the four children, doing very well, and my Larry, *Doctor Larry*, is engaged again! Hope she's not a lemon like the last one..."

"With G-d's help."

"Yes, G-d helps. But, Jerry! I am so lonely without Jerry!"

"I'm so sorry..."

"Yes, well I had to call and comfort you. Not that I'm welcoming you to the club, exactly, but misery does like company, so welcome to the club. If we could go out to lunch, we could be miserable together!"

"Baila, I'm trying to focus on the life that I still have, the fullness of it, not what I'm missing..."

"I know. Takes time to sink in. Call me when you're ready, we'll meet at the Rimon."

"Thanks for calling, Baila."

She was not going to think about it. The emptiness would be deafening, if she listened for it. Loneliness would be maddening, if she let herself into that space. That ominous silence, the absent sound of his heartbeat next to hers. Just call it a warning. A warning that need not lead to panic. Half of you dies—the other half must heal. Some women spend the rest of their lives in silent, or not so silent, suffering.

Does that prove their love? Does that bring peace to the soul of the departed?

Of course not. The opposite, really. The living must get on with life! This acceptance, this continuing to live a purposeful life, brings peace to the soul of the departed, Reva reasoned.

The departed, after all, have no further opportunities to do mitzvahs. They are relying on the living to do mitzvahs in their name.

She missed him.

She reminded herself, again, that one leaves the world when one has completed what one was to accomplish here. Moshe, obviously, completed his assignment.

It was not a comforting thought. It was a sad thought! His opportunities to do mitzvahs were over.

She, on the other hand, had more to do, or she would not be alive here to accomplish it.

Loneliness...

But not always alone. She could feel he was still here, sometimes. She could *feel* that he was here, rooting for her, "Come on, Rev! You're down there now for both of us! You're doing fantastic!" He always was her biggest fan. Strange, that she didn't feel that that had changed...

During the first year, the soul of our loved one is close to us. He was still here, in a way, to comfort her. She gave tzedaka in his name. She wanted to comfort him.

She had to face Shabbat.

They had always had a wonderful Shabbat together, with the children and guests. The children would tell what they learned in school about the week's Torah portion. She also said what she had learned! And Moshe sang *z'miros* in his sweet, tenor voice. Even when he was not so well, even when there were no guests, when it was just the two of them, he made kiddush for her...

Shabbat would be different now.

She received invitations, many kind invitations. People seemed to go out of their way to invite her.

Of course, being nice to a widow is a mitzvah.

But who wants to be a fifth wheel?

Were they just doing the mitzvah, or did they really want her to come?

And since when was she the type to doubt people's motives?

But she felt vulnerable. Alone. *She didn't want pity!*

Who said anyone was *pitying*?

How sensitive she was becoming. She began to go to her children's houses for Shabbat—by Wednesday they were calling her: Ma—where are you going this Shabbat? She began to rotate, give equal time to everyone, a treasured opportunity to see the children and grandchildren.

After Shabbat...

After Shabbat, when she returned home, quiet again. That quiet.

When sadness came over her it didn't overcome her. She would divert her mind to something else.

Yes, the mind can control the emotions. For example, the mind could safely be redirected into memories. And this she did. Sometimes to others, but usually to herself, she would recall the pleasant details of how she and her husband had met, how handsome he was, how she must have looked to him, with her long golden blond hair. She remembered their wedding, his work as a *shochet*, their early years together on the eastern seaboard as their young family grew. How many people they had reached out to and had helped along the way. Young women whose lives they had touched—saved in some cases—

did not forget them. They now had blossoming families of their own, and she was invited to share in their joys, and in some cases, sorrows. She knew widows younger than herself...

She struggled to not be lost in memories.

She woke up one morning, realizing how fast time could creep by. Didn't she have a life? She had her publishing. Legacy Press carried on. Then she received an offer to teach in a seminary in Jerusalem.

And she accepted the offer. To celebrate the new occupation, her daughter-in-law bought her a new watch—an uncommon watch, with two faces, set seven hours apart. The face on the left showed Eastern Standard Time, and marked the minutes as they passed in Brooklyn, New York. The face on the right marked time seven hours earlier—the time as it passed in Jerusalem.

When Reva and Moshe had moved from New Haven to New York, the move was to be their stepping stone to Israel. They finally purchased an apartment in Beit Shemesh.

They never had a chance to live in it together.

So now she had a foothold in each place. Half and half. Which matched, although she hardly ever thought of it like that, a heart split in half.

Switch channels!

From Beit Shemesh the Friday evening sunsets are outstanding. Before lighting Shabbat candles she would be standing on her patio. *Moshe would have enjoyed being here! Seeing this lovely sunset, with music (no siren!) wafting in the hills, to announce Shabbat. Moshe...*

Switch channels!

She was okay. She was fine. She would go inside and light her Shabbat candles.

Every time she brought herself back from the plan-that-wasn't to the plan-that-was, she felt she was making another stitch, stitching up her heart, holding it together.

Stitches hurt!

But she was firm with herself. Life was for the living. Her friend Anna was making a wedding for her daughter. Reva was invited. And she went. She watched as the men danced before the bride and groom...

Oh, how Moshe could dance—his grace, agility—no one could dance as Moshe danced! She and Moshe had met at a friend's wedding, and when Moshe danced, everyone stepped back to watch. Her heart had stopped then. It stopped now as well...

Switch channels!

She left the dancing, returned to her table. Braced herself! No one knew, or had to know, how often she did that. She smiled. She conversed with Anna's sister. No one would ever know!

Six months later, Reva returned from Jerusalem. Six a.m. here is eleven at night there, she checked the watch, not easy to live in two places at one time, no, two different times, that was part of the problem. And today being Wednesday—no, it was Tuesday. Tuesday—Sarah's! She would push herself to Sarah's. Pushing is good. Keeps you busy, keeps you productive, keeps you sane. Now was a new morning. What could she do, *right now*, to help someone *else*? She called Levana, and offered her a ride to Sarah's.

Only two seats were left when they arrived. Reva smiled at everyone wondering how some of the older women, managed to arrive each Tuesday. Neither age nor arthritis prevented souls from coming. The entrée today was baked salmon teriyaki and quinoa. And salads, and Tova's fresh baked challah rolls.

"Part of the lure is lunch," Reva chuckled.

She settled in and focused on Sarah, who had started the discussion.

"And we survived Egypt. Torah tells us how we merited to survive. As we have mentioned before, we did not change three things: our dress, our language and our names."

"Did you ever see how Egyptians dressed?" Davida interjected. "I saw an exhibit at the Brooklyn art museum on dress in Ancient Egypt. They used linen. Real linen. But they made it so fine you could see right through it. Did they wear it like that? I mean, the linen at the exhibit was thousands of years old. Maybe it got transparent over time. So I asked. And yup, that's how they made it from the beginning. Hot climate in Egypt, after all. But the Jewish women wouldn't wear see-through clothing!"

"What about language?" said Yehudis. "Do we speak the same language as the people on the street. You don't even hear a normal sentence. *Like, hey, you, like great, awesome, amazing, whatever like, like!* I think they are losing their faculty of language."

"Speech elevates human beings," Reva found herself saying. "Animals communicate, but human communication, through speech, is not simply instinctive. We transmit ideas, intangibles..."

"True," said Sarah, "Chassidus teaches us that the source of speech is even higher than the source of thought. Doesn't it often happen that when you brainstorm with a friend, you come up with ideas you never would have thought of?"

"Uttering words brings an entity into the world," said Tamar. "Do you know that thinking that you will do something does not obligate you, according to the law. But once you say something, for example, that you intend to make a donation, then you are responsible to do it."

"But once you think of it, you should still do it," said Helen.

"That's a higher level," said Yehudis. "Here we are talking basics."

"Isn't it taught that a good thought is like the deed?" said Faygy,

"Thinking something isn't as good as doing it! The main thing is the deed," said Ora.

"True," said Sarah, "yet if you think to do something, and do all you can to make it happen, but you run up against obstacles that you can't overcome, then we do say the good thought counts as a deed.

"There's a story about Levi Yitzchak of Berdichev," Sarah continued. "He was asked to do something, and replied that he could not. 'Ich ken nisht.' A short while later he overheard a shopkeeper asking a wagon driver to unload the wagon. And the wagon driver replied, 'Ich ken nisht.' And the shopkeeper said, 'You can, but you don't want to!'

"Levi Yitzchak knew that whatever one sees or hears is a message. And here was a message for him: he really could! But he didn't want to!"

Had they done everything they could for Sholom Mordecai? The question passed around the table.

Much creativity went into helping Sholom.

There was the gold drive. Donate your old, broken jewelry, and the proceeds made a small dent in the legal fees.

There was *Sholom Across America*. Thousands of shopping bags with Sholom's picture on them were printed up, and young men volunteered to tour around America, spreading the light of Torah and mitzvahs, and raising money for Sholom.

Now what? Could they perhaps write a sefer Torah—a Torah scroll?

Meanwhile, as Sarah began the entrée buffet, Reva found herself standing next to a young woman who had recently moved with her family to Colorado Springs to establish a Chabad House there. This reminded Reva of the years when she and Moshe were raising their children in Hartford. As Reva and the young woman munched on baked salmon teriyaki, they discussed the challenges of raising children in a smaller town.

"My daughter Shoshanna *still* talks about the little bags of cupcakes she had to take to birthday parties of classmates whose parents did not keep kosher," said Reva. "I would call ahead, find out what they were serving, and send the kosher equivalent. A bar-b-que? Well, hers wouldn't be freshly grilled, but she'd still have a hamburger on a bun! Other girls, whose parents also kept kosher, brought the same little bags. As children, this stretches their limits, yet it strengthened them for life!"

"A man and a woman constitute one soul..." Sarah was beginning to speak, and Reva tuned in.

"Rabbi Akiva taught that Israel was redeemed from Egypt in the merit of the righteous women. What did they do? They went to greet their husbands in the field. The men were exhausted from slaving for pharaoh, so the women brought refreshments. They found small fish in their well water, and they cooked the fish to make a nourishing dish. They washed their husbands, anointed them, gave them food and drink, and had relations with them in a secluded place under the apple trees. They were going to perpetuate the Jewish nation. In the midst of a tortuous exile, they never lost faith in the redemption. In the merit of the faith of these righteous women, the entire nation was redeemed.

"So where does this faith come from? Chassidus teaches us that Women have pure faith because they are directly linked to the Divine will. In fact, in some prayer books, there is a special morning blessing for women, thanking G-d for making them 'according to His will.' Our desire has always been to build the nation. And today as well!"

"Women know how to use their feminine wiles," Reva put in. "It's innate, built into our DNA. Even a little girl can be modest and yet a little coquette."

"The idea is to use this power for the right thing, for the sake of heaven," added Rivka, the matchmaker. "Perfume, oil and makeup go back to Biblical times."

"Her cycle is the source of femininity," continued Sarah. "Before there were intimacy counselors, Torah knew of a woman's needs and commanded the husband to fulfill his wife's intimate desires. You see, it goes both ways. Each husband has a mitzvah to make his wife happy, and this is a very individual thing. He has to learn, and she has to guide him, by day and by night. If he's a *mentch*, they will both be happy."

"Our ancestors were great women," said Davida. "In our generation many are challenged to stay married. They say they're not happy."

"What's 'not happy'?" asked Yehudis. "Is he abusive? Beating, getting drunk, doing drugs, womanizing, gambling? Does he yell, is he controlling? That's abusive."

"Every case is different," said Ora.

"Well, don't just close the door. Sometimes therapy can help," said Tova.

"Try to stick it out. When you lead your children to the *chupah*, you'll see it's worth it," Levana said softly.

"Who wants to be a doormat?" said a voice from the back.

"Taking care of loved ones is not being a doormat," said Levana.

"And if the wife says she doesn't love him anymore?" Same voice from the back.

"Love is a state of mind—making any marriage work—is work!" said Helen.

"Find a redeeming quality in him. Remember all the virtues you saw when you first met him," suggested Tamar, "and magnify them. When was the last time you gave *him* a compliment?"

"You have to work on a marriage," agreed Faygy.

"I'm still at it after twenty-two years!" the voice from the back replied.

"There's always work to do! A growing tree always needs pruning," commented Ora.

"We'll never finish this discussion," said Sarah. "To be continued...!"

* * *

"Shaina, I've got to run. But let's talk for two minutes," said Reva.

"What's up?"

"My friend from LA has been visiting. I've been her chauffeur since last Wednesday."

"Uh huh."

"Well, when this friend lived in Brooklyn, we used to walk on the boardwalk together. She would talk about her husband, a tall, handsome actuary, from Princeton. Unfortunately, after their kids got older, she started comparing her husband to others. This one buys his wife jewelry, that one takes her out every week, this couple vacations so much that they have hardly anywhere left to go! And her husband wasn't as chipper as he used to be. Nothing wrong with her, though. She said she wanted 'more of a life.'"

"So what did you tell her?"

"I said to her, 'Where's your gratitude! For almost two decades, your husband has been toiling faithfully, nine to five, to supply a beautiful home for you and your kids! Isn't *that* interesting? And what are you telling your kids if you split?'"

"Greener lawns are illusions," Shaina agreed. "Everyone I know who jumped the fence landed on burned grass."

"Yes. Thank G-d, she did listen. She listened, she stayed with him, and she's glad she did. But my cousin Lisa had the same kind of story, and she didn't listen. Lisa was married to Steven, the nicest guy. Lived in a palace, furniture gorgeous, had three children. After the youngest had his bar mitzvah, she meets this charmer. I told her to forget it. Stay with your husband! Make a home for your kids. Your husband isn't so interesting? So find a life for yourself. Volunteer, start a business, learn to paint! The world is in front of you! But no. Here was Craig. Craig was her true other half. Craig was her heartbeat and G-d's gift to the world!"

"She left?"

"I told her not to. I told her what the Rebbe said when a woman came to him with such a story. 'I don't love him anymore,' she said. And the Rebbe responded, 'Stop reading romance novels!'

"Lisa couldn't hear me. 'What about me and my happiness?' she insisted. Why should she be longing when happiness is just a divorce away! So she got her divorce, the civil divorce, and the *get*, the Jewish divorce. And oh, happiness! She and Craig could become one."

"Wonderful."

"Two weeks later, Craig had a stroke. A brain tumor. They were able to remove most of it, hoped it wouldn't grow back. After eight months in rehab, he came home, slightly paralyzed. She didn't see how she could marry him now. Somehow the 'true love' had disappeared. Great romance."

"Painful."

"Yes," Reva sighed. "Love is giving, caring, sharing. Give more, love more, and work out the snags. Hopefully come up with a better product."

Be grateful to have a husband to work it out with! she didn't say.

"Shaina, I'd better go. Thanks for listening and sharing."

* * *

As Reva chauffeured her guest, she observed young women walking on the avenue, many pushing double strollers, with a small child or two holding on to the sides. She remembered when....

She was at the end of her pregnancy with Tzvi. And she was anxious. She had managed with three little ones. But four? An infant with *three* other little children to clean up after, teach and care for! How could she possibly?

She heard that a woman in her ninth month could see the Lubavitcher Rebbe without making an appointment. "Moshe, I've got to go to New York. I must tell the Rebbe what I'm feeling—and get a blessing!"

Moshe nodded. He was at her service. He would drive.

"Important for the children to see the face of the tzadik and for the Rebbe to see them," Reva was thinking as the Rebbe's secretary, Rabbi Groner, ushered her family in to the Rebbe's office. The Rebbe greeted them, and Reva began. "Rebbe, after I give birth I don't know what I'll come home to. How will I give to the fourth *and* give to the others..." She spoke it all out, how everything was on her head, how could she do it?!

The Rebbe looked at her, heard her. "You have a good partner," he said and gave his blessing.

Reva said, "I want to thank the Rebbe for his time."

The Rebbe replied, "My time is G-d's time."

She was all smiles as they left. "What a good psychologist!"

Moshe thought that the "good partner" referred to himself.

Only later did Reva realize that the Rebbe had not said "your husband" or "Moshe." A tzadik's words are weighty and measured. Reva understood that the good partner was G-d.

And so it was. She had extra energy. She cleaned and cooked at night, so her days could be free for her growing family. They visited Chatfield Hollow, a lovely lake deep in the Connecticut woods, sandbars at Woodmont Beach, the grassy banks of Indian Wells, the formal gardens of Hubbard Park. Lunch picnics, supper picnics. Didn't miss a beat. She had a good Partner.

Still her Partner.

And didn't it work both ways? When her oldest son got engaged, she looked up to the heavens and smiled. "Thank you, Almighty! And wasn't I a good partner too?"

* * *

Reva couldn't sleep. An old story, not being able to sleep, but this was different. So different! She began to journal, very personal notes, when her son, Eli, called.

People called Eli any time, day, late night, pre-dawn. He was calm, soothing, wise. And if he didn't know what to tell them, he could always ask her.

"Ma..."

"Eli. What are you doing up at this hour?"

"You're up, too."

"Yes, I am."

"I just had to tell you what happened. This guy, Brad, came to us with his ninety-four-year-old mother. She wanted us to call her Bertha—and she was all excited about lighting Shabbat candles and giving tzedaka before she lit them. And when she heard about *Modeh Ani*, she started saying it every morning. She said, at her age, when you get a new day, you really do want to express your thanks."

"Good for her!"

"She even wanted to know about keeping kosher."

"Never too late, is it!"

"Ma, they were joining us every week for Shabbat, but this week they missed. When I called to see how they were—Brad said he was about to call me—his mom had just left this world."

Reva responded with the traditional expression that is said upon hearing that a soul has left this world. "*Boruch Dayan HaEmet.* Blessed is the true judge!"

"Two weeks before her ninety-fifth birthday. She didn't seem so old."

"We've reached the time when a hundred is young."

"Yeah. Ma, Brad says he wants to have her cremated! Even says it's what she wanted."

"Cremated? No! They can't. Not allowed!"

"I'm trying to explain that to him. We've been e-mailing back and forth all night. There's one coming in now. Talk to you later, Ma."

Now surely she couldn't sleep! She prayed that Eli would be able to convince Brad to give his mother a traditional burial according to Torah...

As she lay in bed she forced her mind to more pleasant thoughts. With some effort, she did a complete about face, and landed on a song fragment which frequently drifted through her mind.

Some enchanted evening...

She loved that song. More and more frequently she heard it in her thoughts.

"G-d has many messengers," she thought to herself. "My life is full, and good, and I will wait and see what G-d has in store for me. I am sure that if G-d wants someone for me, someone who is good for me, a soul mate who is not just a roommate, Hashem Himself would be the matchmaker. It would happen!"

These thoughts lulled her to sleep. She awoke in the morning with a new focus.

Feathering the nest.

Her couch was shabby, the chairs worn, the rug faded, the drapes dingy. She hadn't noticed them all the years she had cared for Moshe.

She noticed them now.

Say somebody, say anybody, came to visit her. What would they think? Was she the type who would live in such an apartment? No. She was upbeat and energetic, not worn and shabby! Her apartment needed a make-over! Even for her own state of mind!

After all, doesn't Maimonides say we should surround ourselves with nice things? Coming home should feel good. A home should be relaxing, comfortable, welcoming. And she could do that. She could make a channel for blessings, make her home inviting.

She'd buy a new couch.

And reupholster two chairs, and devise a new color scheme, and find just the right fabric for two new pillows. She'd need coordinating for the wall, and how about a glass door to open on to the deck—may the light shine in!

Said and done. Two weeks later, she had it, and she loved the look. She had set the stage for her new beginning.

The next morning, a flawless sunny day, Reva had arranged to go to Sarah's with her new neighbor and friend, Shira. Reva admired how Shira lovingly and efficiently mothered her large family.

As they walked together Reva commented on Shira's exceptional parenting skills. Shira responded with the story of her marriage and how the family grew.

"No one would believe that I am the mother of ten children," she began. "I can't believe it myself! Sometime I have to pinch myself to believe it's actually me. This is the story of how I found myself in this reality at the age of thirty-six.

"I had not wanted my first marriage to end in divorce, and I struggled for nearly five years to make an ailing relationship work. I davened, I gave tzedaka, I consulted every kind of professional. I tried to change myself until I felt I was an actress reading the wrong script in the wrong play. And my two young children were the captive audience!

"One Saturday night my husband went out. An hour passed, and hours passed, and he did not come home. I felt alone, abandoned, frightened. Did I want to live the rest of my life like this?

"I did not sleep that night, but with dawn came clarity. My mission was not to change him. That was his responsibility. But I was responsible for myself, and for my children.

"So when he came back to the house later that morning, he encountered a new woman. A woman who would no longer beg, or cajole, or be co-dependent. I had removed doubt from my troubled soul, and I felt strong, cleansed, and joyful.

"I was ready to let him go.

"He was relieved as well. He knew he could not become the man I thought I had married. Our goals were fundamentally different. I was committed to family and responsibility, he to self-discovery. And marriage hindered his exploration. We now finally faced the truth.

"The following day I called the Rabbi for an appointment. The word was out! We were bombarded by well-meaning friends, family, clergy, urging us to reconsider. However, this was not a whim, but our effort to heal a deep, festering wound. We were both courageous enough to take this step, confident that we would benefit our family and our future.

"We decided to bypass the bad feelings, resentment and so on that usually accompany a divorce. We would not harbor any negatives toward each other. We would let go of our past, the good and the bad. We would both be free to start a new life.

"It wasn't easy, but we made up our minds and did what had to be done. On Monday morning, after an outing to the ice cream parlor with our two little sons, the divorce was finalized in a Jewish court of law.

"Our emotions would catch up later.

"Now what? The next morning I woke up in my parent's house, in my girlhood bedroom, staring at the familiar wallpaper that my mother had selected especially for me when I was twelve. How strange. I felt loved as a child, yet rejected as a woman. These were feelings that I would have to reconcile in the coming weeks and months. I allowed myself the luxury of crying for love lost. That lasted a full week. Then I was ready to face the world although the mourning would not abate for a full year. I learned how to limit it so it would not encroach upon my life.

"Driving home from work every day was the perfect time to let the tears flow. I could hardly see the road through my tears. I imagined trying to invent a windshield wiper for one's eyes!

"As I mourned I learned to live again. I needed to grow into a new identity, one that could incorporate my entrepreneurial personality. I broke into the business world, and I was successful. I began to breathe easier as my horizons broadened. When I had married, I was eighteen, dependent, and, as I played the role of savior in our relationship, I sank to co-dependency. Now I was becoming an independent individual, preparing indeed to enter the life of my future husband.

"But I am jumping ahead of the story. Torah values determined my path in life, so when I felt ready to marry again, I entered the very efficient, even high tech, system of matchmaking. Oh it is certainly not old fashioned or archaic! Everyone I knew was looking out to find me my Mr. Right! Concerned women formed matchmaking groups, and met specifically for that purpose. At the meetings, everyone presents their list of singles, hoping to set up potential dates.

"If a match shows promise, the investigative stage begins. The singles are not introduced unless there is compatibility in values and goals, and cultural similarities.

"The physical and emotional chemistry, so vital to a thriving relationship, is left for the couple to discover for themselves.

"My cousin, who always had me on her radar screen, mentioned my name to her sister, who mentioned it to her husband, who had a friend that had a brother who recently became a widower at the age of twenty-seven. He had four children, the oldest was six.

"After all the preliminaries we met, and it clicked immediately. Within three dates we were committed to each other and everything and everyone that came along with it.

"When I first saw the picture of those four lovely children, I was hooked. It was a deep intuitive feeling that they belonged with me. It defies rationalization, and I understand that not everyone can relate to this gut reaction, including my family, who were worried about my grasp on reality. On my own I was mothering two young children, and my father felt responsible. He articulated impending disaster. He wasn't going to allow me to make a mistake the second time around!

"I paused to put brain to heart. *Was* I reaching for something that was larger than I could handle? I felt a special energy from Above. It was a very dependable, reliable energy, a knowing from within that this time I would not be left holding the bag alone.

"My first introduction to my family-to-be was to the grandmother of the four children. I was immediately accepted with a loving embrace. How completely and selflessly she accepted me! She was allowing me to take the place of her beloved daughter and become the mother of her grandchildren. Right then I made a silent vow to always welcome this wonderful woman into our home and my heart.

"Now it was my turn to introduce him to my parents. To their credit, it was a complete about face. The moment they met him, my father melted. My mother immediately went on a shopping spree to purchase gifts for her new grandchildren.

"The next five months were spent in deep conversation. The details were not about our wedding plans, but rather about our future family together. We created an ideal vision in our minds of a cohesive family unit. The emphasis was placed primarily on the ultimate good for everyone. Could we all learn to love unconditionally? This was the key. Everything else would fall into place if each one of us was secure in this knowledge. It was clear as daylight to us that if our family dynamics worked, then our marriage would be everlasting.

"We got married. It was wonderful. We spent our honeymoon with the children, and then a couple of days on our own.

"With all our planning and visualization for our utopia, my first challenge became apparent quite soon. In my wildest dreams I couldn't imagine that a sibling picking on another would present drama and dilemma that could undermine our household.

"Had I not lovingly embraced all of my children equally, as we had hoped and planned for so long, I would not have been able to effectively respond to this challenge, which was, in essence, a very common episode of sibling rivalry. This set the tone for our future, because I had firmly established that I loved each child fairly. Thereafter, daily occurrences would be dealt with like in every 'normal' family. It would never be, is it 'his' or 'hers.' All the children are 'ours.'

"Just as are the four children that G-d subsequently blessed us with," Shira concluded.

Reva smiled and nodded. "You brought two halves together to make one whole. You are the woman who represents the ultimate of unconditional love which is hastening the final redemption." Reva and Shira embraced, then entered Sarah's.

* * *

Reva's son Yoni had a loyal cleaning lady named Clara. One day, as Reva concluded her visit with Yoni's family, Clara followed Reva out. Noting Reva's ten-year-old Lumina Chevy, she commented, "You need a new car."

Reva denied it. What was wrong with her Chevy? It goes!

The following week Clara repeated her advice, "You need a new car!"

Reva denied again. "I just got this one fixed. It's working just fine."

A week later, Clara did not change her song. "You need a new car!!"

"Clara! What for? I told you, this works for me!"

"You need a new car! Don't you want to get remarried?!!"

Reva laughed. "If that's the lure, he's not the man!"

* * *

Remarriage. Everyone had strong opinions on this topic. Her children, for example, stood united. After years of caring for their father, their mother was now free. She should stay that way!

"Your mother is still a young woman," commented a friend from Beit Shemesh. "Wouldn't it be nice if she met someone?"

"Oh, she's fine, she's happy the way she is!" the children replied. "She has a life. She doesn't need an old man to take care of!"

And then someone suggested a truly suitable possibility.

Before Reva dreamed of mentioning it, her children sixth-sensed that someone wanted to date their mother! Their grandmother! Four siblings plus grandchildren got on the case.

"Ma! What do you know about this guy? He could be a serial killer!"

"Bubby! I'll check him out for you on line!"

"Where did you find him, Ma? You need this? *You've got us!*"

Yes, it seemed to come out of the blue, from a most obscure source. A woman whom she had once helped in a simple way had a suggestion. And who knows? That "enchanted evening" could be happening. He called...

They spoke for an hour. She liked his voice. She was seventeen years old again, anticipating a first date. And what should she wear!

She was facing a new, open horizon.

"I can't believe that I'm behaving this way. All week long I analyze my feelings. What's with me? How could I, a grandmother, feel like a school girl? The soul—doesn't age! It gets better!"

Marriage! Wasn't this the ideal state? G-d made everything in pairs, even fruits and vegetables have their male and female counterparts. And she had so much to give, and surely someone else out there must feel the same way. Companionship. Giving. Marriage is giving. *Ahavah,* love, is giving...

The next day she visited Shaina.

"Shaina, my friend. I know that what I am about to tell you will not go farther than us."

"I've already forgotten it."

"Well, I got a phone call the other night, and it was a neighbor..."

"Uh, huh."

"Who is close to a particular family—the wife passed away last year."

"Oh. Sorry."

"Yes. So my neighbor asked me if I might be interested in meeting the widower."

"Oh! And you said..."

"I can't believe I said yes!"

"You did!"

"Of course, I hadn't been thinking about remarrying..."

"That's what you have been saying."

"But a nice man, maybe you know the family. Wineman. On Bedford Ave."

"I know that name. Nice family."

"I think so. And I can't believe it! To be in this situation! I haven't gone on a date since I was seventeen."

"Seventeen is a great age for dating."

"Well, of course, what did I know then?"

"So are you going to meet him?"

"We're going out tonight."

"May it go easy for you. They say putting the right two people together is a greater miracle than parting the Red Sea, which, by the way, happens in this week's Torah reading.

"It should be a good sign!"

Chapter Seven
LEAH

Still in Postville, Leah mentally replayed the trial scenes a zillion times.

The proceedings were not held in Iowa.

The judge had determined that an Iowa venue would not be unbiased, because Iowa jurors would have already been subject to media fallout.

It took three attempts by Sholom's lawyers to get this change. Judge Reade finally agreed after a questionnaire sent to 500 potential jurors revealed that 95% had already heard of the case, 75% said their opinions were influenced by the media and 40% had already concluded he was guilty!

She moved the case to Sioux Falls, South Dakota, where the jury would be "less biased."

Where a Jew is rarely seen.

Leah and family packed up and travelled from Postville to Sioux Falls. A group from Brooklyn greeted them, a show of support unexpected by the prosecution. The gallery was so packed that the overflow had to view the proceedings via closed circuit TV in the next room. Leah and Sholom were grateful and touched to see friends who traveled so far to attest to Sholom's character, his legendary generosity and kindness.

Rabbi Moshe Tuvia Lief was among those who came to testify. He spoke of how he had known Sholom since third grade. Sholom's earnestness and sensitivity to the pain of others was evident even then. The packed gallery drank in his words. But the juror's box was empty; Judge Reade had excused them from the courtroom. Testimony of the defense's character witnesses "might influence" the jurors.

A bevy of prosecutors and young assistants buzzed around library carts heaped with thick files. Aaron Rubashkin leaned forward, his face creviced, his hands on his hips as he eyed them. Scenes of Europe, of days better forgotten, flashed through his mind. "Hitler's boys," he muttered.

On the day of the sentencing Leah watched for Sholom. Finally he was brought in, surrounded by iron-faced guards. And he was wearing an orange prison jumpsuit, with his hands and feet shackled! Where did they think he would run! But to demean him, to dehumanize him...

Their efforts failed. Sholom was a prince in prison garb. Look at his face! No one would fathom that he was facing a life sentence.

Life sentence! Leah would not allow herself to think of that! She believed—the entire family believed—that their faith, their trust, their prayers, and the prayers and additional acts of goodness and kindness and tzedaka, given in his merit by thousands of caring souls around the globe—would tilt the scale in his behalf. Surely he would be exonerated, surely this very night he would be freed!

Reade pronounced the verdict. Guilty. Sentenced to twenty-seven years.

The courtroom exploded. The cries of Sholom's sister, Rachel Leah, sounded above all.

"Why are *you* crying?" The words thundered from Sholom. "Why are *you* crying, Rachel Leah? *They* are the ones who should be crying!

"*Shema Yisroel*..." Sholom pronounced the *Shema*, firmly, loudly. He accepted it. He accepted whatever the Almighty willed.

Sholom and Leah's eyes connected.

The courtroom was still in an uproar as the guards took Sholom back to his cell.

That night Sholom was put under suicide watch, standard procedure for inmates who have received harsh sentences with no chance of parole.

The smug triumphant faces of the prosecutors haunted Leah as she packed for the long drive home. What would Sholom's cell be like now? Would he even have a pillow?

But of course this would not be the end. They would appeal.

* * *

Among the mail that Sholom received following the sentencing:

Dear Sholom Mordecai,

My wife has been following your trial proceedings, and has been deeply moved by your faith and the way you have conducted yourself throughout. She has taken upon herself to welcome Shabbat earlier by lighting her Shabbat candles a few minutes before the time on the calendar, and other additional mitzvoth, may their merit assist you in this trying time. She mentions your name in her prayers.

And I myself was astonished by the proceedings. I went to my Rabbi to ask how is it possible for a man to be sentenced so harshly, and at that very moment have the clarity of mind to be concerned about his sister and her cries. How can a person attain this level—to feel another's pain under such circumstances? His rabbi replied, "It must be his study of the holy *Tanya*."*

---

* Tanya: Classic Work of Chabad Chassidus, written by Rabbi Schneur Zalman of Liadi, the Alter Rebbe of Lubavitch

* * *

They did appeal.

Judge Linda Reade was present during the appeal proceedings. "Who ever heard of this!?" demanded Davida.

"The presiding judge didn't find anything wrong! This would never happen in a Jewish court of law!" Reva fumed. "Our courts didn't have juries, someone off the street. We had jurists, learned, honest judges, and they had to hate bribes!"

"The appeal judge and the original judge were all part of the same sham!" Faygy exclaimed.

"We even have proof that Reade helped plan the assault!" Tamar couldn't get over it.

"We've got to go grass roots!" Devorah had another angle. "Look, the White House has this new tack: they want to show how accessible they are, and how the people have a voice! So they promise they will look at any petition that has more than twenty-five thousand signatures! It's all done on the internet—I have the White House site."

This brought great hope to the *Justice for Sholom* supporters. After all, doesn't the President have the power to pardon and commute sentences! The women scrambled for signatures. Reva went door to door, and to events. Mona got signatures after work, and during lunch hours. Aidel telephoned reminders to go online, Rachelle covered everyone in her condo, and Ora didn't let up on this topic during her TeleTorah hour. Meanwhile, husbands stood on busy street corners in Boro Park, Flatbush and Crown Heights. By Purim, long before the deadline, they had over fifty thousand signatures.

Fifty thousand people *daven*ed, hoped, held their breaths.

And from the White House itself, they received a reply: A judicial pardon would not be considered. This is not a matter for the executive branch, stated the official letter, but must be referred back to the justice department.

Who *did* the President pardon?

Devorah had the list. Some drug dealers. Some other thugs and thieves. And one fortunate turkey, who got a stay of execution from a Thanksgiving dinner.

* * *

Leah was grocery shopping just before Shabbat, when Nat Lewin, Sholom's lead appellate attorney, phoned her with news.

"The appeal was denied..."

Denied?!

Leah reeled. Justice? Justice?!! How could—we never expected—how can I tell this to Sholom? And where do we go from here?

Mr. Lewin explained that this news, although distressing, actually put them in a better position. Had the Eighth Circuit granted part of the appeal, Sholom would not likely get a full reversal from a higher court. But since Judge Reade's sentence was completely upheld, another court might grant a new trial.

Leah tried to process this latest happening. The old facts paraded through her mind:

Judge Reade! She never should have been the presiding judge. She had her own agenda. It was no longer a secret that she helped plan the invasion of Postville. During the trial she clearly favored the prosecution—met with them twelve times!—and she withheld information from the defense. And when the defense presented character witnesses, she sent the jury out of the room. Could this be happening in America?

And the sentence! Twenty-seven years for a fifty-one year old man! Because Agriprocessors produced kosher meat? Because Sholom was a Jew, who looked like a Jew, a stereotypical Jew, with long beard, and black coat, as though from the *shtetl*, the way Jews have looked for hundreds of years? What triggered her animosity? What was her agenda? Was it good for her career? The media blows it up and she looks important!

What could Leah do now?

If I tell him that the appeal was denied he'll be dejected. It could ruin his Shabbat.

If I don't tell him, someone else might tell him first. Better it should come from me.

It's not just Sholom! The whole judicial system needs an overhaul. But why does my husband have to be the sacrifice? Why does he have to be the one to prove it!

With the media coverage we've received, the whole world will know about this injustice.

Sholom is strong. He keeps saying faith and trust in G-d, faith and trust in G-d's justice! And with this trust he finds happiness, even in jail.

The next step, Leah knew, was to appeal to the United States Supreme Court.

Chapter Eight
Tamar

"Of all the cases that appeal to the Supreme Court, only about two percent are accepted," Davida had to let everyone know. "They are only interested in universal areas of law that affect the whole country."

"Sholom has the best lawyers," said Ora. "Nat Lewin is on the case, and so is Ronald Rotunda. Alan Dershowitz put in an amicus brief."

"We are putting in our best effort, and thinking positively," said Sarah. "Think good and it will be good. The Almighty will help..."

"That's like a *shidduch*," said Daniela, a young woman who was new at Sarah's. "That's what they tell us about finding one's *bashert*, one's destined one. It's there, waiting for us, but we have to meet people, network, *daven*, work on ourselves—do everything we can do to get it!—and still know that it is not our effort, but Heaven's!"

Another excuse to discuss love and marriage! The topic gave welcome relief.

"One has to be choosy, but not too choosy," Helen began. "Character is what's important. So he has a pedigree? Brains? Learning? Money? He still has to be a *mentch*! And it's the parent's job to find out!"

"I think that the parents ask too much," said Yehudis. "Everyone is so particular. No wonder we have so many singles."

"Detective, yes," said Reva, "but not the FBI and the CIA and the KGB rolled into one!"

"No matter what you do, it's destined who you will marry," said Tova.

"Yet you can't just sit around and wait," said Faygy. "G‑d works within nature, and we have to work within nature. And still it is the Divine Plan."

"Yes, what is meant to happen will happen," said Rachelle. "Did you ever hear the story of King Solomon and his favorite daughter?"

Not everyone had, so Rachelle continued, "This story shows how hard it is to prevent a destined match. King Solomon understood through Divine inspiration that his favorite daughter would marry a pauper from a faraway village. He did not approve. To prevent the match he built a castle for his daughter on a distant deserted island, and sent her there to live.

"Meanwhile the young pauper came of age and left home, seeking a job to help his family. Caught in a downpour, he took shelter in the carcass of an ox, and fell asleep. As he slept, a giant eagle lifted the carcass, with the young man inside, and flew with it over the sea. He set it down on the roof of King Solomon's daughter's castle.

"She was taking her daily walk on the roof, when she discovered the carcass and the young man within it. Of course they took a liking to each other. The young man wrote a marriage contract for the two of them, and the rest is history.

"In time, Solomon came to visit, and saw what had happened. And so the wisest man of the world, who had tried interfering with Divine Providence, blessed the Almighty, and acknowledged that G‑d is the Ruler of the World."

"How are we supposed to know who is the 'right' one?" asked Aidel.

"You have to pray," said Ora. "Pray to meet and recognize him. Also pray to recognize the red flags, which are a hint from Above that this isn't the right one!"

"It's a fine balance," put in Tamar. "Golden vessels require a proper setting. The right one is worth the wait." She was sure of this. She was sure that her daughter, Abigail, would find the right one. She had waited until now, she did not like to think how many years, and they prayed that Abigail's destined partner would show up soon.

* * *

Over the years, Tamar and her daughter Abigail had exciting times together. They visited Israel, they toured Europe. To celebrate Abigail's twenty-ninth birthday, they went on a Kosher Caribbean Cruise. And they had a wonderful time!

Companionship. Friendship. Daughter. Yet more than anything, Tamar longed for Abigail to marry.

Tamar, married to Aaron for over forty years, couldn't imagine life without him. True, they didn't always see eye to eye, but they had become experts in constructive disagreement. Appreciating a different viewpoint helps one to know one's spouse better, and the process of coming to an actual agreement gives the couple a precious opportunity to give and take. She and Aaron were good role models. Eight of their nine children were now married, and were happily raising families of their own. Like *their* own. When parents see their children establishing their own young families on the foundation that they, the parents, have provided, that, thought Tamar, is true *Yiddishe nachas*, real joy.

If only Abigail, now frighteningly close to thirty, would meet her destined partner, Tamar's happiness would be complete.

Of course, Tamar and Abigail did what they could to hasten that day. They helped *other* girls to marry: they *daven*ed for Abigail's single friends, they made showers for Abigail's engaged friends, they secretly contributed funds to help pay for weddings. When you pray for another, G-d first answers you. Not that that was the only reason to pray, of course.

Tamar knew Abigail would be a superb wife.

Marriage was an art, Tamar believed. Marriage was an art that deserved attention. Gourmet cooks got brighter spotlights than gourmet wives.

Gourmet wife. Define it? A wife who can cook up the ultimate in marriage! After all, the pleasures of a great marriage certainly dwarf the pleasures of a good meal! On the other hand, you can enroll in cooking schools to master the art of preparing and presenting foods. It's an art, and can be learned, step by step.

Where is the step by step school that teaches a woman to be a wife, a man to be a husband? Where is the text book that outlines the rules, and where are the diligent students, the qualified teachers?

And should one pass an exam before marriage is permitted?

In Israel, in order to marry, a bride must have a certificate that she studied the Biblical laws of *mikvah*, family purity, and has fulfilled the requirement of going to the *mikvah* before the marriage ceremony.

And in America? Tamar smiled, remembering Reva's description of how, many years ago in Hartford, she would take her fifth grade Hebrew school students on a school trip to the mikvah. "The *Kohen Gadol*, the High Priest of the Holy Temple in Jerusalem, would go to the mikvah on Yom Kippur," Reva would say. "In the mikvah was a specific measurement of pure rain water, and here he would become spiritually purified. And today a *sofer* [scribe], before writing a Torah scroll, sanctifies himself by immersing in the mikvah. So do converts on the day of their conversion. Even new pots and dishes, before they are used for the first time, are dipped into the mikvah pool. And a bride, before her wedding, and thereafter monthly during her marriage, has the beautiful experience of going to the mikvah!"

"I planted seeds," Reva had said. "I made mikvah part of their education. It should be a familiar, normal, modern experience for them, for when they hopefully meet up with it again later in life, the holy laws of Taharas HaMishpacha, family purity."

Yes, there is much to be taught. But the classroom can only accomplish so much. Even more influential are the nuances that children pick up from their parents. These subtleties define who they will become as adults.

Clearly, Tamar believed, it is so important to marry into an appropriate family.

Now without a question Tamar trusted that her daughter Abigail's destined partner existed. To carve out the channel that he should exist as her tangible husband, mother and daughter continued to pray, to give *tzedaka*, and to travel to receive blessings from great holy men and women in the United States and Israel. These are known channels, to help bring down blessings.

They were well occupied. Tamar hoped they had not been so well occupied that they had overlooked the blessing when it came.

A young man pleads with G-d: *Send me my bashert! My destined one. Please! Answer me!*

G-d replies: *I did answer you! Three years ago. What can I do if you only want a size four?*

Another case:

A girl is interested in a particular boy, but her parents convince her that she can "do better." "You'll see, sweetheart. Such a fine girl will find a boy who learns better, who is more G-d-fearing, from a better family, and even with a lot of money!" The girl listened, but never found the boy.

Stories to make you shudder. G-d gives us certain opportunities. We don't know how many. We have to know when to open the door.

Tamar was particularly careful, kept notebooks, and periodically reviewed them, to be certain that a reasonable candidate had not been overlooked. A reasonable, appropriate candidate. Abigail was intelligent, 5'7" and stunningly beautiful, so, reasonably, the boy should be well-learned, and reasonably tall. And from a similar background. A boy whose parents were unfortunately divorced, or who had *Heaven forbid* a child in the family with a genetic disability, just was not appropriate. And Abigail made a nice salary, so it was sensible that her husband should too. No, they weren't looking for a perfect match, just a reasonable one. Although they had not discussed these details recently, Tamar knew Abigail's opinion.

A hard wait. Girls who bloom at eighteen can fade. Not Abigail. Her beauty, like her character, grew ever more refined. Whether at shul or work, she was a modest girl, who dressed and spoke in an appropriate manner. And she had skills. She had a gift for putting things back on track, and she was ever developing her wisdom and compassion. Everyone said so. Hard to find a girl like that—so her other half might also be hard to find! Meanwhile she was making the most of her single years. She became a CPA, worked one year for a neighborhood firm, then landed a choice position with a prestigious company in Manhattan! Not that Tamar would choose such prestige. The firm was secular, the risks were obvious. But Abigail, a woman of discretion, would know when to socialize and when not. Tamar trusted Abigail.

Of course, parents do always need to be aware of with whom their children socialize. Years ago it was easier to track. Years ago they had been a one-phone family. One phone, corded, attached to the kitchen wall and enhanced with a single application: a *ten*-foot (not six-foot or eight-foot) coiled receiver cord, which could be stretched into the hallway, for some semblance of privacy. As household receptionist, Tamar enjoyed pleasant chats with all her children's friends. She knew where her children were going, with whom, and when.

That changed with cell phones. But, thank G-d, she had faith in Abigail.

Where was Abigail now? Tamar was waiting. She should be home soon.

"Hi, Ma!"

"Hello, my love."

She was on that cell phone again. Morning and night Abigail was deeply involved with her phone. Not casual girlfriend conversations, I'll meet you for lunch, or, we'll go to a class together. These were work related apparently, probably deadlines. Millions of dollars could depend on getting the right paper in at the right time. Tamar's husband, also an accountant, had much smaller accounts, of course, but the principles were the same. But so involved? Abigail's whole being was focused, it seemed.

Well, on what else did she have to focus?

However, Tamar had some very good news tonight. A promising *shidduch!* A young man, highly recommended, scholarly, and from an established family. And nice looking. And looking for a girl with the qualities of Abigail. He wouldn't settle for less. Too bad they hadn't met earlier.

Not to get too excited, but one could be hopeful and optimistic. Tamar "lived with the times," lived with the Torah's weekly message. This was the week of chapter *Bo*, when the plagues of grasshoppers, boils, and wild animals descended on Egypt. Tamar thought that just as each plague brought us closer to the redemption, so each date brings one closer to the right one...

This name, Avi Rosen, might be the right one.

"Hi, Mom—I've got this call—excuse me—I'll be back in a minute."

Abigail went to her room, didn't even take off her coat, shut the door. What's so secretive about an office call? Of course, every profession has its standards of privacy.

In Abigail's room, the conversation continued:

"Benny? I'm back—you were saying that it's been a year since she left."

"Yes, and she thought I was going to follow her back to her parents. And I did. I even tried that. Still she wasn't happy."

"You did all you could..."

"She wanted a *get*, the Jewish divorce. So I gave it to her. Yesterday. Every dot dotted according to the law."

"Oh —I'm sorry."

"Don't be sorry. I'm grateful for all your suggestions, all the times you've listened. I tried. Really did. But this is how it worked out. I just wanted you to know. I, I had to tell you. I'm not married to her anymore. I'm not married... to anyone..."

"I'm sorry, Benny."

"Me too. Even after a year..."

"It must hurt a lot."

"It does. But without your help, I couldn't have gone through this and stayed sane. "

"I'm happy I was there to help you. Sorry it had to be for this."

"Yeah. Anyway, thanks. By the way, we still have to do that Lazier and Lefkowitz report. It's due Thursday. Can we meet tomorrow, Abigail, for lunch,—to discuss it?"

"Yes. Okay, Benny. Tomorrow. For lunch... I'm home now—have to go..."

Tamar sat at the dinette table, staring into a cup of strong coffee. She added milk, she even added sugar. A little sugar, she sometimes reasoned, is good. It emphasizes the sweet, the good that's present in everything that happens to us. Everything is for the good.

Rabbi Akiva said that. Reb Zusha of Anipoli said that. The Holy Kabbalah says that and explains: things that appear to us as being not good actually come from a higher spiritual realm than things that are obviously good. We live in a veiled world. What do we know or understand?

We don't understand.

Though we try. Tamar was trying to understand what happened with this match.

This young man, who had seemed to be an answer to their prayers, a scholar, a *mentch* (of fine character), from a fine, supportive family, tall, good looking, with means, what more could they want?

Of course, many offers look good "on paper" but don't hold out through the first meeting. Abigail had had her share of those, and Tamar rationalized her lack of excitement in preparing for this meeting. She looked beautiful, of course. Yet she did not have that glow that girls who hopefully are about to meet their destined partner for the first time typically have. She had more of that glow speaking to her friends on her cell phone!

When Abigail returned that evening, Tamar was up waiting for her. She had not purposefully stayed up, but she was up, so she did wait. Memories of when she first met her husband flashed through her mind. Abigail was her look-alike daughter. Were there not thirty-some years between them, they would have been thought certainly sisters, or even twins. She had worn, she remembered, a blue shirtwaist dress, a cardigan sweater. New shoes. A mistake, those shoes. They had met out of town, on an end-of-the-summer day, at her great-aunt's cottage. A lovely day. They had gone out walking. And her shoes pinched!

But somehow she had walked in those shoes on that beautiful day, when she met this man, who was focused solely on her. How enthralling! Certainly he was the finest creature ever created! Could the feelings possibly be reciprocal?

The magic of one's other half—the fine-sightedness of recognition: that this person is indeed the most perfect ever to be created—for me! Love is not blind. Love is prophetic. Love transcends reason and discerns one's other half.

Such was her first meeting with Aaron Edelson. She once asked him, after they were married, if he remembered those shoes.

"I remember that you looked perfect," he said, "from tip to toe. Everything about you spoke to me—this woman is a woman of valor, you need look no further, here is beauty, fine character, womanly wisdom, you are a fortunate man, Aaron Edelson! And to this day, Tamar, I am still that fortunate man!"

From tip to toe? The shoes had served their purpose.

And to this day she was a fortunate woman. Not that she didn't discover faults. Not that he didn't discover faults! The beauty of marriage was that you have someone who might notice your (own) faults so that you may hopefully correct them. And of course she (and he) also discovered virtues in each other, which being appreciated, became developed. Of course, if you care about someone, and they are discomfited by a fault of yours, you will try to correct it. If you have someone who cares about you, and admires your virtues, you will want to develop those virtues even more. And so, as one climbs from strength to strength, caring about another develops into a deep love, a strong bond between two hearts, minds, psyches and souls. What a fine basis for a bestseller. Such had not yet been written, although one would think that the market would be ready.

Meanwhile, every test to a marriage either makes it or breaks it. Yes, it's work. Children come, there can be health difficulties, problems with livelihood. But if you remember every minute that your spouse is the other half of your soul, (and remember how he was the bridegroom whom you couldn't wait to marry!) then every challenge will serve to make the marriage stronger.

Abigail came home, very unconvinced that this young man was her other half.

"He has many strong points, but I don't think he is for me," she said.

"Can you put your finger on some reason why you wouldn't go out with him at least once more?" Tamar asked, as gently as she could.

"If you feel that it is necessary, Ma..." She would agree as far as that.

"Was she interested?" the matchmaker asked. "The boy felt that she seemed not so interested."

And he's intuitive, thoughtful, and perceptive, thought Tamar. Was it fair to put the young man through one more meeting? Ah, but was it fair not to give Abigail one more chance? Tamar replied that she felt it best that the young people go out one more time. She arranged for the meeting to be the next week, that Abigail should have time to reconsider this young man's many strong points, which would perhaps arouse a stronger interest in the match.

During the week, Abigail glowed more than ever on her cell phone conversations. Perhaps she was reconsidering this fine young man.

Yet on the night of the date, her face, although perfectly made-up, had no glow. And the match was no go.

Tamar did not press Abigail further. If no, then no. She thanked the matchmaker.

The matchmaker immediately called the next name on her list, a fine, not *so* young woman, who became engaged to that fine young man within three weeks.

* * *

Before the seed can sprout, it must disintegrate.

Probably does not hurt the seed. But when unexpected (seeming dire) circumstances necessitate a transformation, this may also begin with silent disintegration. And it can hurt.

Tamar reacted with restraint to Abigail's confidential revelation that she wished to marry Benny. After all, a twenty-nine-year-old daughter is not an eighteen-year-old daughter. Tamar's best efforts to find a husband for Abigail had not materialized. And an opportunity was being offered that Abigail was unwilling to refuse.

Not that Tamar would call Benny an opportunity, but it was Abigail's opinion that mattered here. Different backgrounds. Could these two be compatible?

Abigail came from a religiously observant American household. She was given a fine Torah education. Benny came from a French Moroccan background. His family spoke French, and he had received very little Jewish education. However, as Abigail was quick to emphasize, his level of observance increased after they met. For months, now, Benny had been attending lectures on Jewish topics several nights a week.

One cannot compare such lectures, as fine as they may be, with sit-and-stretch-your-mind-scholarly-Talmudic-study, but Tamar did not at all express this observation.

His background differed from Abigail's in another way. He had married previously and was now divorced. The Jewish divorce, the *get*, had been given. The secular divorce was, according to Abigail, almost complete.

There had been no children from this marriage. Good and not good. How long had they been married? Why had there not been children? And how old was this Benny? Abigail thought he was 32. How old was he *really*? Again, Tamar did not ask.

Tamar did not voice, or even imply, any of these questions. She lost sleep over them, but kept her concerns to herself, and a few close friends.

"Ma, I hope this is okay with you? I mean, I know he's not exactly what you and Daddy had in mind…"

Not exactly.

But if this man was indeed her destined partner, and if he were the man of her dreams, then Abigail should receive her mother's heartfelt blessings.

If he was her destined partner.

Of course, nothing is ever perfect. He is Jewish. She does like him. They enjoy being at the office together.

And at least she would be married.

"Abigail, he does sound like a charming young man. And he shows an interest in learning?"

"Oh he does! That is what we mostly talk about. He just never had the opportunity to learn much beyond his bar mitzvah…"

Tamar wanted to share her feelings regarding Abigail's choice with two close friends. She met with Reva, and together they visited Sarah.

Sarah: In a situation like this, the girl is super-sensitive, especially to criticism. She may see it as a negative unless you welcome him with open arms.

Reva: Give him a chance. There's something about Abigail that he was looking for. Her feelings for Judaism are deep and he never saw that in anyone else. True, he has a late start. But who was a greater teacher and scholar than Rabbi Akiva – and he didn't begin to learn Torah until he was forty!"

Tamar: True, he says he likes learning Torah. Well, he should be going to some more serious classes, not just a lecture now and then.

Reva: I know you were looking for a scholar from Lakewood—but look a little wider. You need to introduce Benny to the right rabbi. One who has not only knowledge, but personality, affability.

Tamar: Yes, but Aaron still wants to convince Abigail to break it off! You're right. That will probably just create bad feelings. I'll have to talk to my husband, and then we can find the right rabbi for Benny. Meanwhile I'll speak to the rest of the family so that we will all be careful not to be patronizing or condescending.

"Be supportive," Sarah summed it up. *"That way, if Benny and Abigail do marry, they will be starting off on the right foot."*

That evening Tamar and Aaron talked it through, once more. Disappointed? Yes. Was this what they had for so long hoped for? No. But this is what Abigail wanted. What was the best they could do now?

They could see what was good about it. Benny was a mentch, with good heart, good character, and pleasant to be with. They hoped he would deepen his commitment as a Jew. Aaron finally summed up their strategy: Benny is a proud Sephardic Jew. When he comes for Shabbat, we'll make sure he fits right in.

Strategically at their Shabbat table was another young man, who worked on Wall Street, and shared Benny's cosmopolitan view. This young man was interested in learning Torah, and attended a class in Manhattan. Would Benny like to try it out? Benny happily agreed.

So Tamar and Aaron put everything they could into place. What was left was to pray for G-d's mercy and Abigail's happiness…

* * *

SOBERING EVENTS IN THE RUBASHKIN CASE:

In the aftermath of the sentencing, the judge determined that no member of the Rubashkin family should ever again be involved with Agriprocessors. Offers of between thirty and forty million had been received for the business. However, bidders backed out when they understood the judge's ruling. Those most familiar with the plant, the Rubashkin family, would not be permitted to show the new owners the ropes.

The bank sold Agri for only nine million dollars.

Agri's freezers alone held eleven million dollars' worth of meat.

Following the trial, the Department of Agriculture formally recognized the prosecutors for their exemplary work.

Following the trial, the town of Postville dwindled to a shadow, and a memory, of what it once had been.

LEAH'S MANTRA

We had the country's top lawyer write an appeal. The appeal didn't work. The petition didn't work. Sholom is still in jail. What do we do now? Aleph, bet, gimmel, faith and trust will bring the geulah, the redemption!

These days, after she moved to Monsey, seeing her husband was a different experience. Every other week, she would drive several hours, to enter a stark building, where the echo of iron gates unlocking before her and relocking behind her chilled her bones. Expressionless guards escorted her to a concrete block visitation room, where bare wooden chairs faced the glass partition which would separate between her and her husband for the one half hour that they were permitted to speak to each other on corded phones.

Despite letters to the federal justice department in Washington from law professors, and senators, and members of the House, and former judges, and despite their petition to the White House, the glaring errors of the state courts were not being addressed. Her now fifty-two-year-old husband remained sentenced for twenty-seven years.

All *davening* affects the physical world. And all Jews are connected. A prayer for one is a prayer for all. Leah wanted people all over the world to pray for her husband, Sholom Mordecai haLevi ben Rivka. That he should be freed from prison.

And may we all be freed from all exiles. As a person. As a people. And as a world.

She would publicize this. Whatever she could do.

A Happiness Conversation

The Divine presence only rests upon one who is happy. With this in mind, the current discussion was how to serve G-d with joy, in not joyful circumstances

"Of course," Devorah was saying, "Anyone can be happy when they are happy. The mitzvah is to be happy whether you feel happy or not. It's a discipline."

"Can you say to someone, be happy, and then—poof, they'll be happy?" asked Yehudis.

"My husband got this mechanical fish for his birthday," said Davida. "The fish opens its mouth and sings, 'Don't worry! Be happy!' Annoying? Yet the kids didn't stop playing it until its batteries ran out."

"It's on the right track," put in Ora. "If you're not worried, you are more or less happy, aren't you?"

"Don't worry, just pray," said Reva.

"Well, there is such a thing as being sad," said Joan.

"Mind over matter," said Reva. "My mother used to say, you have your health, you have your wealth. In Hebrew, the first letters of the Hebrew words *einayim, sheynayim, yodayim ragliayim*—eyes, teeth, hands, feet—spell *osher*, the Hebrew word for wealth! Eyes, teeth, hands, feet—you have it all."

"All the great comedians throughout the ages were Jews," Faygy said. "Court jesters were Jews. All kinds of humor, biting, self-deprecating, social, political, we always had to laugh."

"It's healthy to laugh," said Rachelle. "Everyone should do it a few times a day."

"Just like Eskimos have many words for snow, we have many names for happiness," said Aidel. "Happiness is important, and we have words for every nuance of it."

"Yes," mused Sarah. "For example, *gilah* is the joy of being connected to others, like dancing in a circle of connectedness. *Rinah* is exulting, and *simchah* is the happiness of being attached to G-d. As for being happy when you are not happy," Sarah continued, "well, we always daven for revealed good, for us, for all of our people, and for the whole world. We are always attached to G-d, and we want to feel, be aware of that attachment. When we praise G-d, as we do in the morning prayers, and thank Him with concentration, and meditation, our love for Him becomes our main focus. That pulls us up above whatever negatives are going on, and becomes a channel that influences our situation for good."

"You are referring to the slop pail effect," said Yehudis. "There's a story about Rabbi Elimelech and his brother Reb Zusya that illustrates this."

She continued. "Rabbi Elimelech and his brother Reb Zusya used to wander in self-imposed exile from city to city. One day they were put into prison. The room contained a pail, to be used as a toilet for the prisoners. This depressed Reb Zusya. His brother asked why he was sad.

'I'm sad because I cannot daven [pray]. How can I daven with this stench?! This will be the first time in my life that I'm not able to daven!'

'My brother! Don't be sad. The same G-d that tells us to pray when the room is clean, forbids us to daven here where there is a foul odor.'

'My brother! How happy you have made me!' And the two began to dance with tremendous joy. The other prisoners asked what was going on and they too began to dance! The prison became as joyous as a wedding hall.

'What's going on here!' demanded the prison warden. 'Prisoners, why are you dancing?'

'I didn't start it! He started it!'

'Rejoicing!?'

'Because of the slop bucket!'

'That's why? Then I'm taking it right out!' And he did.

'My brother, now you may daven!'

"And he did."

Chapter Nine
SHAINA

Some believe that they are the universal expert on G-d. People who easily admit that they don't know how birds fly, or how lightning strikes, or even how they digest their morning vitamin, feel that they understand G-d so well that they have a right to tell Him what to do.

From Ora's 6:00 a.m. Tele-Torah-Conference Hour

A subsequent Tuesday at Sarah's, Davida got hold of Shaina's dilemma.

"Cremated!" she shrieked. "No way! I'll tell your aunt why she should *never ever* do it. What's her phone number? She needs to know! Hitler, may his name be erased—he knew! He wanted to wipe out our life in this world—*and in the next,* Heaven forbid! So *he* did that to us. *We* should do it to *ourselves?*"

"People think it's romantic," said Aidel. "Climb a mountain and scatter your beloved's remains over the ocean…"

"Madness," said Tamar.

"How is being made into fish food romantic?" Davida demanded.

"Nothing wrong with a nice old-fashioned Jewish burial," Joan began. "That's what we gave my Charley, twenty years ago, can you believe it! A nice Jewish burial. But in a plain box. That's what the rabbi said. Boxes! You should have seen the boxes they showed me! More beautiful than our dining room set, those boxes! More expensive, too. Oh, I wanted to spend money I didn't have! I wanted to give Charley the best! And then the rabbi, bless him, said a plain box is best for the soul. Our rabbi. Such a wise man. Charley got the best, and I saved a whole year's rent! May he rest in peace."

"A burial is greener," said Chana. "Think how much fuel you have to burn for a…"

"Let's *not* think that," said Tamar.

"Burial is the original recycling," said Ora. "Bury in the ground, and when *techias ha'meisim*, the revival of the dead, comes, we return to life, perfectly renewed."

"I don't know if my Aunt Muri knows about *techias ha'meisim*," muttered Shaina.

"The *luz* bone!" exclaimed Reva. "In the crematoriums, those who had to rake through the ashes, found that the luz, the neck bone, wasn't burned. And now, when forensic scientists need to exhume a grave, they find that same luz bone, intact, to examine for DNA."

"We are made in G-d's image," said Faygy. "Body and soul, both are holy. At this time, the body receives nourishment from the soul. In the future, the soul will be nourished by the body."

"Right," said Davida. "So tell your aunt she can't let herself be burned. You have to do all you can to stop it, Shaina! Even if you have to go to court!"

"People do go to court about this," remarked Tamar. "I just read of a body that has been waiting for over a month for the court's decision!"

"Poor body!" moaned Davida. "It's torture for the soul to wait for burial! But burning would be even worse!"

"My aunt is still living!" insisted Shaina. "Can't we just say tehillim for her…"

"Was her husband cremated? Sometimes couples like the idea of having their ashes mixed together," someone added, helpfully.

"How are we supposed to eat lunch after this conversation?" mumbled Shaina.

"Let's drop it," Reva intervened. "But Shaina, she has to be stopped. Talk to her. Convince her to change her mind."

Muri

As she flew to Plainsview to visit her hospitalized aunt, Shaina rehashed happenings of the past few weeks.

Aunt Muri had not been answering her phone. Muri was always home, alone in that big house. Why wasn't she picking up?

Cousin Dr. Janet called many times from Colorado. Same voice message. Finally she called Muri's niece, Shaina, in Brooklyn. A *niece*, after all, would know what to do.

Shaina got the call just as she was explaining an important matter to her eleven-year-old-son, Dovid, who had Down syndrome. "Dovid, we only call 911 when we *need help*. When we do *not* need *help*, we do *not* call 911. "

"Police!" Dovid insisted. He had discovered that by pressing the 9, the 1 and the 1 again, and then saying "*help*," two of his heroes, real uniformed policeman!—would personally visit his home. Surely his mother understood what this meant to him.

He pleaded. "Police!"

"But you have to really need *help*. It has to be an emergency..."

"Muri might really need help," Cousin Janet was saying. "An emergency..."

"Uh huh," said Shaina, into the phone.

A real emergency. So she called the Plainsview 911.

The obliging Plainsview police department dispatched a patrol car to Muri's. An hour later, they reported that nothing was amiss.

"She answered the door?" questioned Shaina.

"No, ma'am."

"Did you knock the door *down?*"

"Didn't see any reason to do that, ma'am."

"Oh. Well, do you maybe have the numbers of all the hospitals in Plainsview?"

"There are two, ma'am."

The first hospital had no record of a Muriel Jordan. The second hospital asked if Shaina would like to be connected. Mrs. Jordan was a patient on the third floor.

"Hello?"

"Aunt Muri! It's Shaina! So good to hear your voice! Everyone's been trying to reach you!"

"Well, I'm here, darlin'. Not doing terribly well. Came for an outpatient procedure. They botched it up. Can't talk much. Thank you for callin'. Didn't want you folks to worry. So I didn't tell anyone I was here."

* * *

Cousin Dr. Janet called the hospital for the unfortunate details, which she translated into plain English for the family's benefit. "Muri went in for an angio. That's what they do to improve blood flow to the heart. While they were doing it, they had a code blue. That means, she died. So they did CPR to resuscitate her. That worked, but they broke two ribs. So it hurts her to talk. She's frail. Anyway, whatever could be done is being done. She should have surgery, but she'd have to weigh more than 85 pounds to get it. I spoke with her. She insists she wants no visitors."

No visitors? The family mulled this over in their various places of residence, until Diane, Dr. Janet's photo-journalist younger sister, the one who lived in New Mexico with her Navaho Indian husband, announced that she would meet the challenge head on. "Muri doesn't really mean don't visit," claimed Diane. "Even as she speaks, she's probably wondering why no one's shown up. Next week I'm going to Houston, and Plainsview is only ninety miles away." Diane planned to rent a car and hop over.

"She's got guts," acknowledged Shaina.

Diane's guts thinned as she stood outside the neatly tailored grounds of Plainsview Elizabeth Hospital. Should she actually enter? She called Shaina.

"But you're there already," Shaina observed. "You, the famed photo-journalist of the San Paulo massacres, what can stop you now? The worst she can do is throw you out."

Diane entered, visited, and reported. "Okay, she was kind of cool at first, but I went in and I hope I didn't distress her. She asked about the family, and I told her we were all wishing her a speedy recovery. Her lawyer, a Mr. Perry Powel, was there. He says he visits her every day. Here's his number if you want to reach him."

Before she called Lawyer Powel, Shaina wrote to the Lubavitcher Rebbe for a blessing for her aunt's recovery. She slipped her letter into a randomly selected volume of the Rebbe's letters, then opened to the page where her letter was, as is the custom. On that page, she read a response that the Rebbe had written about *sherayim*, the remains of the Rebbe's meal. Shaina sighed, and hoped for a blessing another time. She put the book aside and phoned Mr. Powel.

"Oh, Ah'd say she's doing alright," Powel drawled. "But Ah suggest you come down real soon, if you want to visit with her."

Shaina assured him that she intended to do just that. She'd make arrangements for her children…

"That sounds just fine," said Powel. "Ah see her every day, and she is hanging in there, but it would be good if you would come down. Bah the way, Mrs. Jordan has written, and Ah do have a copy in her own handwriting, that she wants her remains to be cremated. Just thought you should know."

Cremated. Remains...

In a flash, the Rebbe's letter became relevant: the issue indeed was remains, what to do to a Jewish body that *remains* after the soul has left it. Clearly she must follow Jewish law. When the time came—may it be many years from now—Aunt Muri must not burn.

* * *

Shaina couldn't understand why Muri would want to. Who in the family ever considered such a thing? Although Shaina came from a family that was not yet fully Torah observant, as far as Shaina knew, all family members who had left this world had opted for a Jewish burial. Lifestyles may vary, but at end cycle, everyone had turned to the tradition. She called Reva.

"Huh, you think! Unfortunately, people do it," said Reva. "My son Eli dealt with such case recently. Brad's mother Bertha. They e-mailed back and forth the whole night. I'll forward you pertinent parts of their dialogue."

She did:

Dear Rabbi,

It's so hard for me to write about this.

I don't know if you understand that this is what my mother wanted. She thought it was a beautiful custom that her remains be kept near her loved ones, well, that is, me. Now she can be with me all the time. I don't have to go to some cold cemetery. She doesn't have to go into the cold ground.

I'm crying as I write this. Can't go on.

Brad

Dear Brad,

My heart goes out to you. And on top of everything, when your heart wants to grieve, your head must make decisions.

Where your mom is now, she understands, and deeply wants and needs a Jewish burial. For the first year after death, the soul and body are still connected closely. It's a time of transition for the soul, from being in a body, to which it has become attached, to enjoying the truth and pleasures of the spiritual realms. G-d has given us directions so we can make this transition in a way that will comfort the soul, who feels a double pain. It has pain at being separated from us. And it also feels our pain, at being separated from it. By comforting the soul of our loved one, we in turn find comfort.

The One who created the soul and body gave us explicit directions as to how it should be laid to rest. It would be my honor to take care of all the details for your mother, who so much enjoyed doing the mitzvahs as she discovered them. The whole process of preparing the body for burial and burying the body is a profound mitzvah. Your mother's soul would now have great pleasure from your keeping this mitzvah, and allowing her to keep it.

With comfort,

Eli

Dear Rabbi,

I read your letter. I can't sleep. I can't believe my mother is gone. Last night she was fine! She had a cup of soup and some cooked pears. I think that was the last thing she ate in this world. She looked up which blessings to say, too. She was saying blessings on everything. "Look what G-d is giving me!" she said, like a kid unwrapping a present. Yeah, she had this thing lately about thanking G-d. She didn't have much appetite, but she'd eat a bite just to thank G-d for it.

She saw the truth in that. She also saw the truth in leaving the land for the living, who need it. Why should she take up a plot of land for eternity, just to lie there dead in it? I remember her saying that, 20, 30 years ago. Even though we did bury my father, that's not what she wants. It's her last wish! I want to honor her last wish! Isn't that a mitzvah, too?

Brad

Dear Brad,

I feel so privileged to hear how your mother spent her last days—thanking G-d! If only we would all use our time so well!

Of course, I can see why your mother wanted land for the living. Certainly we would rather have parks than cemeteries! But the One who created the earth designated how it should be used. And we find that Abraham, the first Jew, was very careful to bury his wife Sarah, and even paid a fortune to purchase the burial site at the Cave of Machpela. Today, Sarah's spirit is still there to listen to the prayers of all of her descendants who come to daven at her grave. And so it will be, until the time, may it be very soon, when all bodies will come to life again, which according to Jewish belief will happen after Moshiach comes, which we expect every minute.

In the meantime, we have the mitzvah, the G-dly commandment, to prepare the holy body of your mother in a very beautiful way, and bury it as all our foremothers have been buried since our mother Sarah.

If your mother were aware of this tradition, and the beauty and importance of it, she would certainly want this and only this. I am here for you twenty-four hours a day.

Eli

Dear Rabbi,

My poor mom! I'm just thinking of it now. Why should she be stuck having her spirit mourning around her body. Let the body be cremated. And she'll be free!

Brad.

Dear Brad,

Your dear mother was grabbing mitzvahs as fast as she could find them. What an extraordinary woman she was—to kosher her kitchen at ninety-four years old! My wife is telling me that she even went to the mikvah! That single immersion will have a far-reaching effect on all her descendants, and indeed on our entire nation.

Brad, the mitzvah of a Jewish burial is the one mitzvah that your mother has left. Mitzvahs nourish the soul. You see how she was hungering for mitzvahs. Certainly you will honor her soul, and her memory, by giving her a traditional, Jewish burial.

I'm here for you. E-mail me or call me any time.

Eli

Dear Rabbi,

If anyone else were keeping me up at this hour after a day like I've had, I would turn my computer off and go to sleep.

I can't sleep anyway.

I have to think about what my mom really wants. I can't even hold my head up. How about calling this a night?

Brad

Dear Brad,

You need to keep up your strength. I also can't sleep. So call me whenever you can.

Eli

The e-mails ended there.

Shaina texted Reva. "Anything happen after that?"

Reva's reply: "Funeral was the next day, thank G-d."

* * *

Last Purim, Shaina had sent her aunt a Purim gift, a box of Purim treats. Muri called back to say that she enjoyed the chocolates.

That was their most positive religious conversation.

Unfortunately, Shaina's rare but well-meaning attempts to encourage anyone in her family to participate in mitzvahs weren't so well received. Family members held dear to their right to personally customize their own religious experience. When Shaina once suggested the beautiful custom of lighting Shabbat candles, the response was curt: "Don't tell us what to do."

After that, Shaina didn't.

There are in the world, however, others who are more persistent. Young men, wearing black jackets and black hats, weekly walk the streets of Manhattan and elsewhere, armed with *tefilin* (prayer straps). Week after week they visit businesses, and offices. Relentlessly they inquire if the Jewish businessmen there would like to put on tefilin.

If the answer is affirmative, they will assist in winding the straps, and in saying the appropriate prayers.

If the answer is negative, they will try again the next week.

And for as many weeks as it will take. For weeks, for months. Even years.

And at some point, all the stories go, Mr. Businessman has a change of heart. Facing a financial crises, or serious illness, or desperately wishing to have a child, he succumbs to the possibility— to the necessity!—of Divine assistance.

And his prayers are answered. Unbelievable as it may seem, countless accounts testify that the mitzvah had an effect. The beloved, for whom the doctors had given up all hope, revives. Finances, languishing at bottom line, take a blessed upturn. Or miraculously—a pregnancy. And all because the young men with the prayer straps did not give up. Words that come from the heart enter the heart, and a Jewish soul never gives up on his fellow Jew.

Shaina discovered that as private as Muri usually was, she did share her end of life preferences with her brother, her sister-in-law, her rabbi, and her lawyer. In fact, she told everyone, except Shaina.

Nor did anyone else tell Shaina.

Understandably.

But why did Muri want cremation?

Shaina had looked at a book on the topic by Doron Kornbluth. The cremation industry, the business of cremation and its operation, is described, detail by graphic detail. The amount of fuel consumed, and the processing and disposal of bone fragments and metal body parts were among the topics mentioned. As Chassidic texts conclude, from what has been already stated, "the wise will understand."

As far as Shaina knew, no one in her family had ever wanted this, although a few, unfortunately, had had these services performed for them by the Nazis in Auschwitz. What was Muri thinking? Wouldn't she want to be buried next to her husband?

Or had he had the same idea?

Uncle Jerome never seemed the type to buck tradition. Nevertheless, Shaina called her father. Uncle Jerome had had a funeral, hadn't he? He was buried, wasn't he?

Gelfarb admitted that although he and Shaina's mother had flown to Planesview for the funeral, they had arrived too late to attend the graveside service. He had supposed there had been one. Why wouldn't there have been?

Aunt Paula also assumed that Uncle Jerome had been buried. Always had thought so, although she didn't know it to be a fact. However, Jerome's sister's husband, Manny Tessler, would know for sure. A fine man, Manny. His wife had passed away a few years ago.

Shaina called Mr. Tessler, who was happy to tell her about the family. Yes, of course there had been a funeral. Before Jerome passed away, he had expressed his desire to be buried in the family plot. His space there was waiting for him. When his parents had purchased their places, they had also bought one for him.

If something, uh, happened to Muri, asked Shaina, couldn't she be buried next to him?

Well, not exactly, replied Tessler. Being that Jerome's plot was in the corner of that section of the cemetery, near the road, there was no adjacent space. When his folks selected this particular piece of land, Jerome was solidly single and over fifty. At that time, a stretch of three plots seemed appropriate.

Tessler continued. Yes, he knew Muri wanted to be cremated. And he knew that wasn't according to the Jewish way. But it was what she wanted. So what he hoped to do, he confided to Shaina, was to gather her ashes and bury them in Jerome's plot. There were regulations on this sort of thing. Tessler was willing to deal with the regulations.

Shaina persisted. In that section of the cemetery, was there no vacancy at all?

Oh, there certainly was, Tessler affirmed. Two rows up, and four places down, sort of catty-corner from Jerome, may he rest in peace, was an available space.

Tessler clearly knew the territory.

Okay, thought Shaina. Cremation was not the Jewish way. But was it really so bad? Unpalatable in this world. What about the next?

She called Rabbi Shea Hecht, son of Rabbi J.J. Hecht, who had been one of the right-hand people of the Lubavitcher Rebbe.

"So bad?" she asked.

"Worse. Were it my aunt, I'd do anything. Go to court. Everything. Give her a Jewish burial, Shaina. Don't let her burn."

* * *

Mr. Powel called a number of times over the next few weeks, suggesting to Shaina that now and not later would be a good time to visit.

When should she go? She could have left any time. But Shaina, among many others, did have the custom of "writing to the Rebbe" for a blessing before setting out on a journey. On almost every page of her volume of Rebbe letters, blessings could be found.

As it happened, blessings were not found on any of the pages that Shaina opened to.

"You haven't left yet?" asked Reva.

"No blessing yet," asked Reva.

Reva was not a fan of this type of letter writing. But she couldn't argue with the Baal Shem Tov's teaching that everything is by Divine Providence and no thing is coincidental.

Chanukah passed, and so did Tu B'Shvat, the new year for the trees, before Shaina opened to a "blessing letter."

She would later realize that her timing was perfect.

Her flight was perfect, too. As the Delta jet soared into the crystal sky, Shaina witnessed an impeccable view of the world below. Winter no longer froze the earth, yet still no hint of spring. Bare patchwork fields flanked with shadowy hills chilled to the end of February. A grayish thread, the Mississippi River, starkly divided east and west. So clear was her plane's eye view of earth! If time could have such transparency, what would she see?

She felt as though she dangled from a bungee cord, high above the vast unknown.

Why is time so much less transparent than space?

G-d knows what we will do, but He does not make choices for us. Our prayers and actions shape future into present. We are royalty upon the earth, not G-d's pawns.

Those were Shaina's thoughts, perhaps elevated by altitude. When she landed, she would have to push thought into deed.

She hadn't seen her aunt for ten years.

How *would* she accomplish this mission? She didn't have Davida's passionate persistence. Or Reva's understanding of human nature. Or Tamar's well-reasoned logic. And certainly not Sarah's armory of knowledge and wisdom. What was she? A simple soldier, with the Rebbe's marching orders calling on her to show up.

They landed in Houston. Shaina navigated the airport, boarded a twenty-four seater propeller shuttle plane to the Plainsview Airport, where she was directed to a wiry man who wore, yes, really he did wear, cowboy hat and boots. His car service would take her to Elizabeth Hospital.

Muri was in the east wing, the "hospital within a hospital," the receptionist said. How it was different from the hospital that was not within a hospital? Shaina was afraid to ask. In Chassidus the inside always connected to the higher spiritual level, while the outside linked to the lower spiritual level. That may not have been the reference here. The receptionist guided her to the elevators, and Shaina was whisked away to the shadowy, vast and carpeted fourth floor.

No hospital smell, yet the air felt heavy. Shaina noticed a small crucifix hanging from a wall in each room. Sixty years ago, the nurses here were nuns.

Mrs. Muriel Jordan was printed on a small card inserted in the name slot outside room 411.

Shaina was used to seeing her aunt's name on the little cards that directed you to the table assigned for your dining pleasure at family weddings and bar mitzvahs. Mrs. Muriel and Dr. Jerome Jordan. Her childhood family was for always, she had thought. Like the cornerstone of a building. Her own assignment may have been to grace an upper floor, but she had always thought that the cornerstones would stay as they were, forever.

No cornerstone belonged in the hushed halls of Elizabeth Hospital.

She reminded herself that she was now an adult, with nearly teenaged children, and a husband who had recently become a member of the AARP.

In Muri's presence, she felt five years old.

"Aunt Muri—it's Shaina."

"Oh. Shaina."

Oh. Shaina. Was that a welcome? At least it wasn't a dismissal. Her aunt seemed not surprised that she came.

"I —I wanted see you..."

"I'm not... so well..." her aunt dozed off.

"She sleeps a lot," said Chrysanthemum, the day aide. "But I gave her a bath today, and washed her hair." Chrysanthemum smiled. "Miz Jordan likes it when I fix her hair."

Indeed, her aunt's hair, grayish white, straight, and stiff, was neatly combed.

"It—looks very nice," commented Shaina, although of course it didn't. Where was her aunt's real hair, that bounced and danced, framing her vibrant face...

"Water!" her aunt startled awake and was demanding. Chrysanthemum hurriedly handed Ms. Jordan a paper cup of water and ice chips. Her aunt sipped and settled back in her pillows.

Chrysanthemum looked at Shaina. "So you are Ms. Jordan's niece? Have you seen Mr. Powel yet? He visits here every day."

He visited within the hour. A white-haired gentleman, over eighty, she understood, but nearly six feet tall, and unbent, introduced himself to Shaina, holding out his hand.

Shaina greeted him with a smile, and apology, "Happy to meet you, Mr. Powel—uh—it's just that Orthodox Jewish women don't shake hands with men."

"Oh!" He withdrew his hand as though it would have touched fire. Shaina just continued to smile, a response which usually resolved this awkward situation. There had been a discussion at Sarah's regarding shaking hands with men:

Aliza (who sold insurance): Wear gloves. I think there may be an opinion that it's alright for a woman to shake hands with men if she is wearing gloves.

Esther (real estate): What's wrong with shaking hands? Better than embarrassing people.

Zina (interior decorator): My mama says if it's not yours, don't touch it.

Reva: It's a male thing to shake hands. Women kiss. And a touch is not *just* a touch. To touch someone is meaningful. Not just sensual. It has feelings behind it—should have feelings behind it. Sends messages. Otherwise what's the point!

Davida: Who has to be embarrassed? Just tell 'em. Torah says: men and women don't touch, unless they are parents and children or spouses. Nothing personal. Makes sense, doesn't it? Think of all the problems we'd solve if everyone did it this way!

Shaina favored Davida's approach, less abruptly, of course. Smile, explain easily, and if anyone cared to know more, she'd gladly tell them.

Powel actually was interested. At lease he was interested, to sit down at the end of the hallway, in the puffy upholstered chairs, for some friendly, relaxed conversation. Relaxed! Plainsview wasn't Brooklyn.

"The senior partner in the first law firm Ah worked for was Jewish," Attorney Powel began. "Yes, he was Jewish, taught me the ropes, taught me everything Ah knew. He was Jewish, and when we'd go out for lunch, he liked ham sandwiches. That's what he used to order."

"There must have been a lot of assimilation in Plainsview," replied Shaina. "But if he had had a real chance to learn Torah, he would have liked it. You would also like it. That's where laws come from, you know. From the Torah. You should see the Talmud, full of legal discussions. You think a law book is big! A volume of the Talmud is three, four times the size, with small print, and even smaller print, different commentaries, running up and down around the edges. You have to remember the relationships between five or six things just to learn a seventh. You'd like it, Mr. Powel. Takes a head and makes a head to learn Talmud."

Powel nodded attentively, especially when Shaina added that she was a former law student.

"You were!" He was pleased.

"Won 100% of my cases," Shaina added. "One out of one. I helped a woman win a pro se divorce."

"Contested?"

"No."

"So that's nothing."

"Wasn't nothing to her. She got her divorce. After twenty years, too."

Powell lifted his eyebrows, and changed the subject. "Your aunt's a fine woman. My wife and I have been close with the Jordan family for many years. I knew Jerome's parents."

"Oh! That's how you know Muri." The family had been wondering how Mr. Powel knew Muri and why he was so attentive. Matter resolved.

"Yes, and she made her wishes known to me, and I wanted to make them known to you, too. Here is a copy of her hand-written directives. I have the original at the office."

"*Remains are to be cremated. Broussard's will be fine. Do not give in to family protests.*"

Followed by her aunt's signature. A little larger, not quite so firm, as the *love, Aunt Muri* signature on the Chanukah cards she always sent. Yes, a little shaky, but her aunt's signature nonetheless.

"This is from three years ago," observed Shaina. "She might have changed her mind."

Powel smiled. "Your aunt's wishes are well known, and these are her current wishes. She has not changed her mind, nor do I believe she will."

Another gentleman, also tall, but more athletic than the portly Powel, was coming down the hospital hallway. This was Muri's brother-in-law, Manny Tessler. He wore a navy and white jogging suit, and jogged, or bicycled, daily. He was eighty-six years old.

Tessler welcomed Shaina warmly, also offering his hand, but Powel corrected him.

"You can have this copy," were Powel's parting words to Shaina.

Tessler sat down in the chair vacated by Powel. "I won't go in her room," he said gently. "Once I did and she threw me out. I just check up on her from here."

"That's really nice of you," said Shaina.

"Well, I'm all the family she's got, here in Plainsview," said Tessler. "I do what I can do. How is your family, Shaina? I remember your parents. They came up here a few times."

"My mother, may she rest in peace, passed away just about three years ago. My father is recovering from a hip replacement. He's doing okay."

"Yes, I'm sorry. I remember hearing about your mother. My condolences. I'm glad to hear that your father is well. How long are you staying here?"

"As long as necessary."

He nodded. "That's good, very good. Where will you stay?"

"Oh, I'll just be here, at the hospital, with my aunt."

"You could stay at your aunt's house, if you want to. Powel has the key." He saw that Shaina didn't want to leave. "Well, is there is anything I can help you with? Maybe you need to go shopping?"

"Thanks. I brought supplies with me, but I may need to replenish."

"Just call me. And give me your cell number as well."

Before he left Tessler repeated his ashes-in-the-gravesite-of-the-husband solution, adding that he was prepared to get whatever special permit was needed.

"Thank you," said Shana, "But I hope that won't be necessary."

Tessler nodded, as though neither he nor Shaina wanted to admit the inevitable. He wished Shaina good night, repeating that he would help however he could.

When he left, Shaina called Rabbi Moshe Traxler, in Houston, who was known to be familiar with end of life issues. He urged Shaina to speak with Muri, adding. "My son Mendy and Rabbi Goldstein will be in Plainsview tomorrow to visit the prisons. There's a huge prison complex near Plainsview, and we try to visit there every month. After the prison, they'll try to stop over to talk to your aunt."

They come once a month, and the day they are coming is tomorrow. Good timing, thank G-d, thought Shaina.

Shaina prepared for The Discussion with her aunt. She opened her Tehillim to say a few psalms first. *G-d is my shepherd, I shall not want... as I walk in the shadow of death...* Apparently G-d knew where she was.

But Shaina was intercepted before she reached her aunt's room.

A tall woman (apparently everyone in Texas was tall) wearing rhinestone-encrusted sunglasses introduced herself as Rabbi Susan, rabbi of Plainview's only local Jewish House of Worship, Temple Shalom. The women shook hands.

"I appreciate your coming to see my aunt," said Shaina.

"I come to visit your aunt as often as I can," replied Rabbi Susan. "But I have so many other obligations. In fact, I have a baby-naming in less than an hour."

"Oh, that's nice," said Shaina. "I'm glad the community here is growing."

"Yes. Well, your aunt is a woman of strong opinions. We all knew that—I guess you know that. We try to respect her opinion, especially her last wishes. I'll try to stop by again tomorrow."

Shaina didn't respond to this. No need to start up now. After all, this was Susan's turf.

But this was Shaina's aunt.

That evening, Shaina dined on canned sardines, and mulled over the fact that she had not yet had The Talk. Hopefully tomorrow. She spread a hospital sheet over the reclining chair which would be her bed for the night. Her aunt slept stiffly, only lightly covered, and the room was cold. Why couldn't they get Muri a nice warm quilt? On the other hand, she was sleeping deeply. Maybe she was comfortable enough.

Vicki, the night attendant, was curling up in a blue knitted afghan, watching TV. Shaina, who rarely watched television, was unfamiliar with this show where insensitive critics panned the performances of young hopefuls—to their faces. Shaina didn't like it. The young people were talented. And the judge's criticism was not only rude, but too vague to be helpful "You know, you just didn't, didn't have what it takes tonight, Eric." Would young Eric ever attempt guitar again? Could he see through the assault to the desire to entertain that launched it? Yet Eric smiled through it all! The barbs bounced off. Shaina wasn't desensitized, took it personally for him...

She could get lulled into this, focusing on someone else's reality, escaping her own.

She forced her mind elsewhere. Review facts. Her aunt was still living. Her aunt could live until one hundred and twenty years old!

Determined to speak with Muri in the morning, Shaina fell asleep.

* * *

And awoke early. Vicki was gathering up her afghan ready to head out, while Chrysanthemum settled in for the day, armed with a cream donut. Muri also awoke early, grumbled as her blood pressure was taken, and acknowledged her breakfast trays by pushing them away. Chrysanthemum got clearance from Shaina to dash down to the cafeteria for a cup of coffee.

Alone with her aunt, Shaina attempted the first meaningful conversation that they ever had.

What Shaina said was something to the effect that mitzvahs give life, that even *agreeing* to do a mitzvah could make one live longer, in better health, and that even agreeing not to do something that was the opposite of a Torah commandment could also add productive time to one's life. Muri seemed interested until she understood which mitzvah Shaina was referring to. Then her eyes blazed. "No! No! Go away!"

"I'm not going away, Aunt Muri. I love you. I want you to stay here, with us."

In retrospect, Shaina could not recall if she actually said this, or just thought it. Shaina had never contradicted Muri. She had never seen Muri's tough side. She was seeing it now.

Only outwardly does a Jew not want to do a mitzvah, Sarah had said many times. Inwardly, yes, inwardly mitzvahs are what every Jew wants to do. Every Jew wants to connect with the Almighty, and mitzvahs are the way.

Muri, lying in the hospital bed, looked frail, frail with an iron core. What would change her mind?

The truth, thought Shaina. Meet up with truth, and there is no other opinion.

Truth is relative. Her cousin Diane would say that.

Truth is relative to other levels of truth, but truth is still truth. And relativism is not an excuse for anything-goes-ism. She would reply something like that. She settled into saying the morning prayers and waiting for her afternoon visitors.

Rabbi Goldstein, tall (of course) and slim, with an elegant red beard, and Mendy Traxler, younger, less ruddy, but also tall, arrived around two o'clock. To Shaina black hats and beards never looked so good—they appeared as though they had stepped right out of Crown Heights. *As a ship-wrecked survivor greets his rescue ship, so I...* she imagined writing something of the sort in her diary. Goldstein, meanwhile, observed that the room had a wall decoration.

"I had covered it up," said Shaina. "Someone must have uncovered it."

"I think it's a little loose," said Goldstein. It did indeed easily detach from the wall. "Wouldn't want it to fall and break," he added, as he tucked it into the back of a drawer, and joined young Traxler at Muri's bedside. Together the two men said Psalms.

If only we knew the power of Tehillim, the previous Lubavitcher Rebbe had written. Shaina felt that she was in the midst of a symphony. Surely her aunt felt the holiness pulsating through the hospital room. Right here in Plainsview! Shaina leaned over her aunt. "Aunt Muri!" She addressed her aunt loudly enough for Goldstein and Traxler to hear. "Whenever the time comes, may it be many years from now, you do want to have a Jewish burial, don't you!"

Muri agreed. Goldstein and Traxler were witnesses.

As her aunt dozed off again, her visitors slipped quietly out of the room with Shaina.

"Write up what you saw," said Shaina, "that my Aunt agreed to a Jewish burial. Get it notarized. And fax it to me here."

The young rabbis agreed, and wished Shaina a complete recovery for her aunt.

Muri's physician, Dr. Harlan, tall, slim, merciful, and determined, also yet hoped for Muri's recovery.

"She is still alive!" he stated. "We are not taking her off sustenance."

But Muri spoke little the rest of the day. Occasionally she made some high pitched sounds, which Chrysanthemum deciphered. "Water, Ms. Jordan? Here's some water. There. Isn't that nice!"

Muri made the sound again. This time Chrysanthemum determined that she wanted her pillows adjusted. Meanwhile Tessler called, asking Shaina if she wished to shop for groceries. Seemed like a good time to take a break. Shaina accepted the offer.

Manny Tessler's cream-colored Lexus was a comfort, as was Tessler himself. They reached the nearby Krogers, a mega-grocery that could easily swallow the six commercial blocks of Kingston

Avenue. Oh for the short familiar aisle of Raskin's Fruits and Vegetables! Shaina began the grocery trek, confronting fifty varieties of everything from applesauce to Ziploc bags. She located kosher sardines, a few more necessities, paid, and longed to return home to Crown Heights.

Tessler dropped her off in front of the hospital. Grey skies, mild weather. Shaina tried to imagine spring. The hospital had a bit of garden. Shaina found a stone bench, romantically situated under what might, in a month or so, be a flowering something. She sat down, wondering how many young nuns had also been there, contemplating their future.

"You don't have to give up having a family to serve G-d," she would tell them. "Look in your Bible. Be fruitful and multiply. G-d said it. G-d likes us to have children. That's how we best serve Him! You ought to try it. We show our love to G-d by getting married and having big families and raising our kids to be people-loving, G-d-fearing adults." These thoughts she sent out to the universe. Some young nuns might catch them and take heed.

Yes, husband and children. She missed her husband Shmuel, and she missed her daughter Chana and her son Dovid. She thought of the Rebbe, and wrote down her feelings. Aunt Muri could live for a long time yet, and she was homesick.

She put her note into a book of the Rebbe's letters, and looked at the page that she had opened to.

A footnote. About how the soul of Jew or non-Jew suffers if the body is cremated.

She would not ever, *ever*, let that happen to her aunt.

The air chilled, and raindrops began to splatter on the open page. Shaina hurried into the hospital, just as Rabbi Susan was dashing into the corridor. "I've been looking for you. The doctor says your aunt is dying. I've already said the final prayers with her."

Shaina ran to her aunt's room. Chrysanthemum was there, so was Powel. Rabbi Susan stood at the foot of the bed, Shaina stood at her aunt's right side. Muri was breathing, with difficulty. She seemed unconscious. "I love you, Aunt Muri," Shaina whispered. All eyes were on her aunt, who breathed out with a sort of shudder.

"That's it," said Chrysanthemum. "That's it!" As a hospital attendant, she was familiar with last moments.

"Let the doctor decide," stated Rabbi Susan.

The doctor entered, his face somehow whiter than Muri's. He prodded his stethoscope, urging it to locate the sound of life. There was none. Dr. Harlan shook his head. He took it hard, he always did, always felt personally responsible for death. He considered for the umpteenth time transferring into stem cell research.

"Blessed be the True Judge," said Shaina.

"Well," sighed Powel. "May she rest in peace. I guess the funeral home will come for her now…"

"But she is not to be cremated," interjected Shaina.

"But those were her wishes," said Powel.

"She has changed her mind," stated Shaina. "She has changed her mind in front of two rabbis. They wrote out a statement that they witnessed her change of mind, and they had the document notarized. I have a fax of that document." She handed Powel the statement.

"This is worth nothing," said Powel.

"The court will decide," said Shaina.

One has no clue from old Texan westerns how nice the people of Texas are. Polite, considerate, and refined. Not really the pistol-drawing type, from what Shaina could see. And the epitome of this refinement was the director of the Broussard Funeral Home, Charles Dickens.

Yes, that is his real name.

A name easily remembered. Shaina couldn't resist asking him if he was related to, but he wasn't, and Shaina immediately regretted asking a question he had undoubtedly endured a zillion times. Any other first name would have been okay. On the other hand, perhaps Charles was a traditional name for the Broussard family. Charles' mother was a Broussard.

Charles Dickens was impeccable. Impeccable in grooming, dress, and manners, and not more than thirty-six years old, Shaina figured. Dark suit, white shirt, but young and healthy looking. Not like the tall, thin, sallow, shadowy, grey-haired, grey-skinned gentleman, who visited the hospice after her mother passed away. He had seemed to be Finality itself. But with Charles there was something vibrant, something hopeful. Even though funerals had been the Broussard family business since 1886, you could imagine Charles, after hours, having a nice family picnic with his wife and kids.

He went by the book, exactly. There were six Broussard locations in the greater Plainsview area, but the body of the deceased would be taken to the nearest one, not far away. Shaina would later find, to her relief, that the cremation equipment was housed at a different facility. It seemed, in fact, out of character that individuals as well-bred as the Broussards would stoop to do cremations. If they would know the spiritual ramifications, Shaina was certain that they would discontinue the service.

"By Jewish law, there must always be someone in the room of the deceased," she informed Mr. Dickens. "It's called a *shomer*. I will be the shomer."

Dickens, who had great respect for customs, had already heard of this one, and told Shaina that she would be welcome as their guest at the funeral home. Exiting the hospital though a basement back door, they passed quickly through the chilly morgue, where nothing eerie happened. A black vehicle was waiting for them. Shaina's aunt was taken to the back of the vehicle, and Shaina sat in the front. The drive to the funeral home was eight short blocks.

They paused by the back entrance. Attendants popped out from somewhere, to transport the deceased through wide doors, up an immaculate elevator, into one of the sitting rooms of the funeral parlor.

This sitting room would be Shaina's home for as long as she remained in Plainsview.

"You might be more comfortable downstairs," suggested Mr. Dickens. "It's a larger room, a bigger couch…"

"Thank you," Shaina replied firmly. She would be with her aunt. "I'm okay here."

"The sitting rooms, chapels, offices and so on are on the first floor," he added.

Shaina nodded. He made everything seem so normal. As though being in a place where not-living people were was dignified, and not creepy.

And wasn't that how it should be? Dickens and the attendants left, and Shaina was alone with Muri.

Their sitting room was quiet. Muri's casket was covered with a quilted maroon blanket.

Shaina had also been offered blankets, which she had graciously refused.

"Everything is okay here," Shaina thought to herself as she *davened* the afternoon and evening services. *Blessed be You, G-d, King of Eternity, Who brings to life those who are dead.* This prayer, recited three times a day by Jews all over the world, is found in the *Shemoneh Esrei*, the most sacred part of the prayer service. Here a clear point is made: Death is just a temporary interruption of G-d's original plans for eternal life.

The body is designed to come back to life, and this belief is one of Maimonides' Thirteen Principles of Jewish faith. Shaina concentrated hard on these words, hoping that her aunt might tune in on her prayers and be comforted.

Someone knocked.

No reason to be alarmed. Shaina opened the door. Her visitor, a living woman, introduced herself as a Broussard employee. Was there anything she could do for Shaina? They would be locking up around ten, and an alarm system, hooked up to the local police department, would be activated for the night. In the morning, someone comes to open at six.

Shaina understood that the only living person at Broussard's that night would be Shaina.

She nodded and thanked the woman.

Of course, G-d is everywhere. Shaina concentrated on the comfortable features of the room, the upholstered furniture and coordinating draperies, as she prepared for bed. As she said the bedtime prayers, she especially noticed the references to G-d's protection.

...the Guardian of Israel neither slumbers nor sleeps...When you lie down you will not be afraid, you will lie down and your sleep will be sweet.

Shaina was amazed by how peacefully she slept.

She awoke early, expressed her morning prayers, had breakfast. Really, she had nothing else to do here, until the meeting with Mr. Dickens, Mr. Powel, Rabbi Susan and the executives of her aunt's estate. She had plenty of time to pray, and "guard" her aunt.

Her company arrived promptly, and everyone was pleasant and civil. Charles Dickens carried a large manual, and brought folding chairs to accommodate everyone. Powel greeted Shaina, and introduced her to a slender elderly gentleman, Mr. Ben Woodhead, who represented the bank as executor of her aunt's estate. Manny Tessler greeted Shaina. He was the other executor. Across from Shaina sat Rabbi Susan, wearing black trousers, black jacket, and black yarmulke. Shaina smiled at all.

The initial discussion was whether Muri had really changed her mind. Susan, who professed to know Muri well, felt that Muri had *not* changed her mind. Tessler added that he was not aware of any change of final wishes. Powel commented on the fact that only Shaina and her rabbi friends were informed of this change of heart, so close to her aunt's passing. It was suspect.

"What happened is what happened," said Shaina, without elaboration. "My aunt wants a burial. I will not leave her side till she gets it, and I will go to court if necessary."

Mr. Woodhead put the tips of his fingers together, bowed his head, and listened sympathetically. He and Powel spoke a few words.

"That is true," said Powel. "My power of attorney ended when Muri passed away."

"And our power as executors of the estate will not begin for several weeks," said Tessler, "until it is approved by the court."

Dickens nodded. "Last night I consulted with the senior members of our funeral home, as well as with the funeral home association laws and regulations. In a case such as this, we are informed that the final decision is made by the next of kin. Does the deceased have children?"

No. The deceased did not. But she had a brother who was yet living—Shaina's father, Mr. Gelfarb. Perhaps he could be reached by telephone?

He could. Shaina had spoken earlier to her father to relate the unfortunate news. Her father responded that he had hoped to see his sister before she left this world. He had reservations for a flight the next morning. Unfortunately, his sister had not been able to wait for his arrival. He would be forty-eight hours too late.

Shaina contacted her father again now. "Hi, Daddy. I'm at the funeral home. There are a lot of people here who want to talk to you."

She handed the phone to Dickens. "I'm going to put the phone on speaker, Mr. Gelfarb." Dickens introduced everyone present, and explained the purpose of the assembly.

"I see," said Gelfarb. "Well, I would like to hear what everyone has to say."

That won him a lot of points. Gelfarb, a man in his mid-eighties, clearly had all his marbles. Tessler, the rabbi, and Powel all presented their viewpoints. "Do you think she changed her mind?" Powel asked Gelfarb.

Gelfarb's words were measured. "Knowing my sister," he said, "and knowing my daughter—and her rabbi friends—I tend to think that she did not."

Tessler, Powel, and Susan nodded approvingly.

"But that is a decision that I will make," Gelfarb continued, "when I arrive in Plainsview. I am scheduled to be there tomorrow afternoon."

* * *

Gelfarb, like the better men of his generation, was a man of values, not opinions. Even his well-known preference for the Cleveland Indians was not an opinion—the Indians were, to be sure, his *home* team, and supporting the home, and what it represents, was a value deeply etched in Gelfarb's heart.

As the eldest son of a traveling salesman, young Gelfarb took his responsibilities seriously. While still a student in Coventry Elementary School, he awoke before dawn to stoke the coal furnace so that his mother and "sis" (Muri) should wake up to a warm home.

After his father's untimely passing, he worked in an iron factory to help support the family. Later, with the war brewing, and a younger brother to fill his shoes, Gelfarb received permission from his mother to enlist in the army. The Second World War had peaked, and was beginning to wind down. Gelfarb was assigned a machine gun, and was stationed in the Philippines to "wipe up."

He couldn't help observing that the "enemy" here consisted of a few scattered young Asians, who most certainly had mothers, and perhaps also fiancées, back home. As much as Gelfarb was a patriot first, he valued all humanity as a close second. He was relieved that in the thick of the fray, he could not confirm the destination of his bullets.

His active duty career was brief. His most memorable skirmish was with native hot peppers, and he learned the hard way not to use them as a condiment for his mess kit (a story Gelfarb would write up sixty years later for the *Wadsworth Gazette's Senior Page*). Soon after this event, Private Gelfarb came down with a mysterious ailment. The illness remained undiagnosed, even as he was shipped to a California hospital where he wasted away until the war ended. Fortunately, shortly after Victory Day, the illness was happily identified and quickly remedied. Gelfarb, pronounced cured, returned home to Cleveland to be fattened up by his mother and his wife-to-be.

Gelfarb's pure trust in doctors and ability to appreciate hospital amenities, the fresh linens, the meals in bed, the nurses on call, enabled him, in the course of his lifetime, to survive a number of hospital stays. Whether the distressed organ was lung, heart, colon, stomach, kidneys, or the necessity of replacing one or the other of his worn-out hips, Gelfarb persevered. He had recently completed the rehab for his second hip replacement when his sister unfortunately passed away.

"Daddy, are you sure you can travel?"

"Of course I can travel."

He could and would. And even if he couldn't, he wouldn't accept help from Shaina. But he would accept, in fact he would expect, dinner. Fortunately, he also liked sardines.

Shaina lit Shabbat candles, wondering how many more Shabbats she would be spending at Broussard's. She prayed for the soul of her aunt, the body of her father, and for her own strength. She suddenly felt overwhelmingly tired, and went to rest on the sofa...

Soon after she closed her eyes, she experienced a *bang!* inside her head. In her mind's eye she saw an owl, dressed as a policemen, holding a club in his wing, pursuing a small bird, the soul of her aunt, whose wings clung to its body and could not fly. The police owl chased the little bird down a sort of funnel, around and down, around and down, down, down. Where does this end—thought Shaina. But she saw no end...

Shaina startled awake, and felt deeply recharged. Nothing would stop her from protecting the soul of her aunt.

And now she had a visitor.

"Ah don't see why you're so against cremation." Powel had dropped by to say hello, hoping to meet Gelfarb, who had apparently been delayed. "Although Ah personally would never consider it, those were your aunt's wishes."

Powel shrugged, and then continued. "At any rate, the executors of the estate have decided that they don't want to go to court. Your father is next of kin, and we will abide by his decision."

"Oh," said Shaina. No comment, no commitment.

"I would advise you," said Powel, "to do the same."

Powel left, took the stairs, just missing the sound of the elevator chugging up. With only a few minutes until Shabbat, the double doors opened, and Gelfarb, wide-eyed, leaning on his cane, faced his daughter.

"Come in, Daddy. Good Shabbat."

She treated him to a full course meal. The heat-retaining styrofoam cups had indeed cooked the kasha. They also transformed the baby spinach into spinach "soup," and of course there were the stalwart sardines. Shaina had brought challah rolls and grape juice with her from Crown Heights. Her father made kiddush—he always did make kiddush—and they washed for the challahs. The coffee table served for dining. Something about her father—wherever he sat became a throne, wherever he was became a palace.

After the meal, he leaned back on the upholstered chair and sighed. "I was hungry," he said simply. "On the plane they only offered peanuts. Do you sleep here?"

"I'm the shomer. I'm watching Aunt Muri."

Gelfarb looked around. "Where...?"

Shaina motioned to a door next to the elevator. "That door leads into a cooled room. After 24 hours those still here have to go there."

Gelfarb barely winced. "I wanted to get here before... but alright, I didn't."

"Do you want to sleep here? The Broussards are very hospitable. There's a larger room downstairs."

"Tonight I have reservations in a nearby hotel. I'm pretty tired."

"Of course. Well, I hope you'll get a good night's rest."

He would need it.

The following day Shaina had another meal prepared for her father. Like Queen Esther preparing for King Achashveirosh—two feasts before she made her request. Esther saved the entire Jewish nation, Shaina wanted to save one soul. The sages say every soul is a whole world.

Gelfarb ate and Shaina discussed several lines of thought with him. Yes, he saw that just as a poem requires a poet, and a picture implies a painter, so the Universe implies a Creator. And yes, it could be, that just as an automobile comes with a manual, so that it may be used and enjoyed properly and fully, it could be that the Creator also gave humankind some sort of manual, to help direct an optimal life.

The Torah? So be it, the Torah. And G-d cares about every decision that everyone makes? Perhaps He does. But G-d also gave men minds. No doubt He expected men to use these minds, to use their own judgment and decide a great deal on their own.

"Honey, I don't believe she changed her mind. Everyone knew what she wanted. If she indicated some change in her final hours, she was either pressured against her will or she was groggy and not really herself. Her real final wishes need to be followed. Anyway, right now I need a nap."

He stretched out on the couch. Shaina said Tehillim, occasionally peeking in on the other side of the door, to check up on her aunt. The room was not scary, just dark and predictably cold. Her visits were brief.

Father and daughter understood that The Topic would not be discussed until after Shabbat.

Gelfarb made *Havdalah*, escorting out the Shabbat queen. Shaina prepared tea and the remaining challah, for the *Melaveh Malkah*. The Shabbat Queen, the feeling of Shabbat, would stay a bit longer.

"Alright," said her father. "I'm listening."

"She changed her mind," said Shaina simply.

"I don't believe it."

"She did."

"Hmm. You told her something?"

Shaina offered explanations. The Torah. The Kabbalah. Not good for the soul. Since the time of Adam, who saw a bird burying its dead and so knew what to do with the body of his son Abel, since then a Jew buries…

"You can tell me that. You couldn't tell her that."

"She was more sensitive to this information then. She was leaving the world…"

"If she was leaving the world, she was in no state of mind to make a decision."

"A dying person is not allowed to change their mind?"

"So how come only you—you and your rabbi friends—knew about it?"

"Daddy, you need to inform yourself as much as possible. Maybe there are some people you would like to talk to?"

"My rabbi. The rabbi in Akron. I'd talk to him. But I don't have his number."

"I have it. G for Rabbi Grunfast." Shaina had spoken to Rabbi Grunfast when her mother passed away.

But the rabbi was out of town. A recorded message said he would return the next week.

"I'll speak to the cantor, then," said Gelfarb. Everyone loved the cantor. Shaina hoped for good advice.

The cantor was happy to listen to Gelfarb. After a quarter of an hour, however, he could only admit that nothing he had learned in his cantorial studies had prepared him to counsel on this topic, although he did not think that cremation was the Jewish way.

"I see. My decision. Well, thank you, cantor. Funny—I was kind of hoping that you would tell me what to do."

Gelfarb looked at Shaina. "Nope. And I don't think she changed her mind."

"Daddy, talk with our friend, Dr. Levi Reiter. He has a degree in psychology and works with a lot of older people." She gave him the phone number and left the room.

The conversation was lengthy. "So it can be," concluded Gelfarb, "that people might change their mind just before death. But, my sister? I can't see it."

Shaina had others in her arsenal. Rabbi Gluck of Agudah of New York, after offering an array of cogent arguments assured Gelfarb that if it was a matter of money, he would pay for the funeral himself.

It was not a matter of money. Gelfarb expressed his appreciation for the rabbi's time, then turned to Shaina and announced that he would go to sleep. Too late to return to the hotel. The first floor room at Broussard's would be fine. Shaina didn't press her father for a verdict.

Shaina woke up at five the next morning, dressed, davened, made her way down the wide curving stairs. Her father was on the phone, speaking with Dickens. Arrangements...

"What...?" Shaina interrupted the conversation.

"Honey, she did not change her mind. The car is waiting for me and I have a plane to catch."

"Daddy, don't decide anything yet. Let's talk."

"Alright!" His voice was gruff. He told Dickens he would call back shortly.

How did her father's mind work? What could she say that would reach him?

"She did change her mind," said Shaina, gently.

"She didn't," stated her father. He looked at her closely. "Why does this mean so much to you?"

In a rare moment of insight, Shaina replied, "Why does it mean so much to you?"

"Because this is what she wanted."

"No, Daddy. *This* is what she wanted."

Father. Daughter. Eyes met.

"Alright!"

Softly, "Thank you, Daddy."

Dickens arrived, and spoke privately with Gelfarb in the sitting room. Shaina overheard "plot" and "perhaps Tuesday." Today was Sunday. Why the delay? Seconds later, her father hurried from the sitting room, took his luggage, left Broussard's, hardly acknowledging his daughter. His strength was declining, his balance questionable, but his determination was strong. He descended the steps of the funeral home without assistance. He would say his farewells to his sister from the limousine waiting for him at the end of the driveway. He was not waiting for the funeral.

Shaina watched her father, royal, sitting like a king, in the back seat of the limousine.

May he never become old, Shaina thought. *May he live and be healthy forever.*

Without allowing thoughts to melt into emotions, Shaina turned to Dickens and asked what the burial procedure would be. He replied that this must be arranged by the Temple's burial society together with the cemetery director. Neither would be available until Monday.

"She's waited long enough," said Shaina.

Dickens nodded professionally, which was not without compassion. However, nothing more could be done today and he was already late for church. Shaina called Rabbi Traxler.

"Wonderful. Good work, Shaina. Now you need a *tahara*, the preparation before burial. Here are some numbers. I'll also call. We'll see if we can get some ladies together."

"They said that the *levayah* won't be before Tuesday."

But it was. Eight o'clock Monday morning, Dickens was pleased to tell Shaina that the funeral would be at two that afternoon.

Levayah means to accompany. The body, and the soul which yet clings to it, is accompanied by loved ones to the burial site, where the soul receives a sendoff with Psalms and prayers. This mitzvah of accompanying the body is considered the epitome of true kindness, for here is a favor that cannot be repaid. Before the levaya is the mitzvah called the *taharah*, the purification and preparation of the body, performed by the *Chevra Kadisha* (literally "holy society") of each community.

Plainsview had once had a Chevra Kadisha. Shaina was referred to Dora Horowitz, a woman in her late seventies, who remembered when her mother was a member. "I am so sorry to hear that your aunt has passed away," said Dora. "She was a wonderful woman. Now we just let Broussards do the preparations. Ask them about it."

Shaina was impressed that the ever-accommodating Broussard's stocked burial garments straight from the heart of Borough Park. "Good," said Traxler. "Kosher shrouds. I've found two ladies from here who can do it. But postpone the funeral until three."

"We really can't wait past two," said Dickens.

Shaina pushed. "Is it overtime?"

It was. "No problem," said Shaina. "Add it to the bill."

Joyce and Ruth appeared, like angels, from Houston. They embraced her, with gentleness and sympathy, as though Shaina was newly bereaved.

As *though* bereaved? *Wasn't* she bereaved? Her aunt was no longer alive in this world!

But there was no time to think of that now. Her aunt was still very much in this world; she was at this very moment in the very next room awaiting her taharah. "We really need three people," said Joyce. Shaina braced herself to become the third.

She had no clue how.

"We'll show you," said Ruth. "Do you mind if we read the prayers in English? English is better for us, but we do have the Hebrew alongside, if that's better for you."

"G-d knows all languages," said Shaina, feeling grateful for all prayers.

What happens in the room of the taharah is generally discussed only by members of the Chevra Kadisha, who are especially trained for these final preparations. They are a select group, quiet, modest, almost secretive; they don't advertise their membership. As Shaina entered the purification room, she could almost feel the sanctity of the proceedings.

The garments were white, unwrinkled, flawless, and the tahara was conducted with exceeding gentleness, care, and modesty. Even the water used for washing was warm, out of respect for the departed. The garments were tied in a special way, to form the Hebrew letters *shin* and *dalet*. The body itself, said Ruth, is the *Yud*. Shin, Dalet, Yud spelled G-d's holy Name.

Shaina had chosen the coffin, as unadorned as Broussard's could supply. They didn't carry the more simple models, but the one she selected was made entirely of wood.

That was the main requirement.

One other detail. Shaina had asked Rabbi Susan, please, for a *minyan*—ten Jewish men—to be present at the funeral, to say *Kaddish*, the short but holy prayer that sanctified the name of G-d. This would also assist her aunt's soul on its journey.

"We are an egalitarian congregation," said Susan.

"We need ten men," Shaina repeated.

"I'll see what I can do," was the reply.

Appropriately, the weather was coldish, cloudy, a dampness that didn't quite drizzle. At the cemetery, Shaina found the hole that had been dug for her aunt's grave. And it was already nearly filled—with muddy red, clayish, water!

"Happens all the time," a Broussard attendant explained. "We're at sea level, you know. They'll pump it out."

A canopy and folding chairs were provided for the more than ten men, plus women, who attended. The service would be short, as Muriel had wanted as little ceremony as possible.

Shaina did not object. They would have a chapter or so of Psalms, and Kaddish with ten men. Nothing else was required.

The casket was lowered, and sand sprinkled on. After everyone shoveled their symbolic spade-full, Shaina herself covered the casket completely with sand, as she had been advised. Then the crew stepped in to replace the clayish mud.

As the congregation filed out, only Dora Horowitz introduced herself to Shaina and again expressed regrets.

The attendant from Broussard's remained, standing at a respectful distance, moseying around. He was expecting Shaina to take her time.

Shaina faced her aunt. Clay mud did not smell like fresh earth, but that's what this locale had. The body of Adam, the first man, was composed of earth from all over the globe, so that his body would be accepted for burial in any location. Shaina had never considered that fact especially soothing, and she was surprised to find some comfort in it now.

"Well, Aunt Muri, thank G-d, it's done."

Silence. What did she expect?

Shaina read a few chapters of *tehillim* in Hebrew, hoping that this offering would grace her aunt's journey. The workers had dismantled the canopy, and all that remained of the funeral was the great mound of mud. Shaina looked up to the damp sky, and felt a chill that penetrated earth deep. Then she remembered that her Uncle Jerome, Muri's husband, was buried nearby. Two rows down, and four places over, sort of catty-corner from Muri, was Jerome's location, may he rest in peace.

Shaina stepped over to his grave, to say *tehillim* for him as well. She remembered him, a dear gentleman, who never spoke an unkind word. She remembered the day that he and her aunt married and she remembered how Muri packed her trousseau, a small suitcase, but so carefully prepared, to join her husband, after their wedding…

Suddenly, Shaina experienced a bright light, and an infusion of happiness and elation. The larger than life presence of her uncle, his warmth, his smile, beaming, with gratitude and joy. She heard his voice—without sound, but *his voice: Muri's here with us now, Shaina. Muri's here now. Don't you worry. Everything will be just fine!*

Shaina finally allowed herself to weep.

Chapter Ten
ORA

5:30 a.m. The sun will dawn any minute, yet the moments before dawn are actually the deepest, darkest part of the night. Ora is up, sliding into robe and slippers, making her way over the immaculate granite floor to her spacious breakfast nook, which also served as the Torah Teleconference's dedicated office. Her phone, an antiquated corded model with its large and well-lit key pad, awaited her.

Ten minutes to go. Since she had founded her Torah Teleconference several years ago, Ora had not let a weekday pass without addressing her callers from the comfort of her breakfast nook. Other Torah teleconferences existed, but hers was the only one for women at 6:30 a.m. She always opened with a cheerful welcome, mentioned a local event or two, then launched into some insights on the weekly Torah reading.

And today should be a real winner. The drama of the Exodus. As the moderator she would say:

The prophets reveal that G-d says: "I remember the kindness of your youth—you followed Me like a trusting young bride [out of Egypt] into the desert, to a barren land." That is to our credit, forever.

"Where we find ourselves now," Ora would say, "is more than three thousand three hundred years from that liberation. We are guaranteed that this exile will be our last!

"Never mind that some have their eyes on our Temple Mount.

"Never mind that they've even built a mosque on it, excavated under it, claimed they have a right to it, and plot to annex it.

"Everyone knows that the land of Israel is promised to the Jewish people. We have the deed.

"Is a tenant assuming more right than the landlord?

"We, the children of Jacob, are returning to our roots!

"The apparent rise of our enemies, and their unmitigated *chutzpa*, is simply another sign of the imminent arrival of the Moshiach!"

And she would continue:

"The final moments before the redemption are called the end of days—the end of the days of exile. We are standing in those final moments now.

"What acts of goodness and kindness can we do to hasten these days?"

Then she would open the floor to the listeners, and hear what the women had to say. Those who were unfortunately not able to call in at 6:30 a.m. could hear the conference at any time by calling another number.

Really, it was a lot like Sarah's table, with all the technical advantages of broadcasting by phone. It was also, of course, more public. Her husband often warned her not to be too controversial.

This morning Sarah was joining her as the guest speaker. News was already out that Sholom's Supreme Court appeal had been denied. Sarah would no doubt touch on this. She connected Sarah and began,

"My dear telephone listeners, it is my great pleasure to introduce Sarah. She is my teacher and so much of what I say here comes from her. 'If an unhappy thought comes knocking, don't let it in!' is from Sarah, and so is 'Giving, doing, being there for others makes us feel good about ourselves.' Sarah? You're on the air."

"Thank you, Ora! You know, the mitzvah of to *love your neighbor as yourself* is a basic essential to our lives as Jews. It's our foundation.

And we can ask, loving ourselves is one thing. But how do we love someone else like ourselves?

"The Hebrew words themselves show us how. The word for neighbor here is 'raya' which actually means a chard—a piece of a vessel. For the vessel to be whole, we need all the pieces. Each piece has its own place, its own role in making the vessel whole. My piece needs your piece.

"This vessel is made of every Jew since the beginning of time. We may manifest differently and separately. But our souls are linked and intertwined, we each are infused with an actual part of G-d, and we are spiritually designed to work together, to become one body, united and holy. We are not complete without each other.

"How greatly do I see this since the imprisonment of my brother. Every day we get letters from Jews all over the world, sending us support and encouragement. As though *their* brother was imprisoned.

"We are all brothers and sisters.

"So I want to thank you. You who share my pain, I would like you to also share my happiness. People wonder how I can be happy after I've heard my brother's verdict. And after the Supreme Court has denied our appeal. A *habeas corpus* appeal is our last legal resort.

"Should we look worried?

"I'm sure I don't have to tell you that worrying doesn't help! It helps to remember that the word itself explains its meaning.

"The Hebrew word for worry—*DA-AGAH* is spelled with the four of the first five letters of the Hebrew alphabet: it has an Aleph, Gimmel, Dalet, and Hei.

"It does not have the letter Bet. Why is the *bet* missing?

"Because bet stands for the word bitachon—which means trust. When you have bitachon, trust in the Almighty, there is no possibility of worry!

"Happiness leads us out of our limitations, and ultimately lifts us out of the situation that was pulling us down. G-d's Divine Presence only rests on us when we are happy. We know that we are not alone, we are never powerless. G-d is here with us and He answers our prayers.

"Since we are one vessel, we long to daven for each other. And so we ask everyone to please remember Sholom Mordecai haLevi ben Rivka in your prayers, as well as anyone else who needs salvation, healing, shidduchim, livelihood. Please do a good deed in Sholom's merit and for all of us, and may all our prayers and acts of kindness bring the redemption, for us all, immediately."

Ora concluded, "Thank you so much, Sarah! Our time is up. Listeners, please join us again tomorrow!"

Chapter Eight

RICHIE THE CELLMATE

Richie, a contractor from Nicaragua, learned it all on the job, learned electric, plumbing, building, architecture, water proofing, and he didn't mind getting his hands dirty as long as his pants stayed clean. He'd wear white pants, too, white pants, even down in a pit. Richie wasn't just anyone, he was a cut above. He could talk about it, too, about how his grandfather owned thousands of Nicaraguan acres, and a hacienda, not exactly true, but he could tell it like it was. Richie was good at telling, not that he was educated, but he was smart, more than smart. He had the brain of a building genius, he could fix houses, even build them from the underground up. He *knew*, that was it, knew buildings, from his gut. No amount of education could teach you like that. Contractors subcontracted to him, he wasn't legal but he was cheap, cheap and better, cheap and the best! On the side, he'd pocket some cash or jewelry, more than made up the difference. Rich ladies wouldn't miss a ring or two. Usually he didn't get caught.

Well, sometimes he did get caught, caught with the goods, or near enough to them, not often, but it happened, and here it just happened again. So he was here, back in prison, the most G-d-forsaken one he'd seen yet. He'd heard of great correctional institutions. That's what they call them in this country, *correctional institutions.* He had even heard of a prison in St. Louis where each cell comes with a TV. Inmates there get counselors for group discussions, and if you're an artist you get to paint murals on the walls. Now *that* is a prison worth getting convicted for, why didn't they build them all like that! TV! How sweet time would pass with a TV! What was his sentence this time? With a TV he'd know what day and time it was, he'd know the news of the world, he'd hear of worse tragedies than what happened to him.

Hurricanes that left Haitians homeless, hungry and bad hurt, that was a story, he followed that one, until the news people got tired of reporting on it. Japan's tsunami, that was a story, buses, cars and boats, all colliding together like bathtub toys jamming up as the water goes down the drain. Sometimes they speak about volcanoes erupting, or who knows, these days, it could snow in a desert, or heat up in Alaska, maybe, could be, strange things were happening, and it's good stories that make clocks move. But here even an ant crawling on the floor is an event, something different to look at, breaking the monotony of the concrete floor, steel bars, dirty ceiling, iron cot.

And a Jew. You don't get any choice of roommates here, unless they figured it into the system, worse crime, worse roommate. Did they ever think of that, to assign you roommates according to your punishment? But this guy was in for twenty-seven years! Heavy. How much jewelry do you have to pocket for twenty-seven years?

Well, he, Richie, would rather be with this twenty-seven year guy than with some of the crazy-makers out there that he'd seen. Mix a crazy with a not crazy, you'll soon get two crazies—he'd been there when that happened. The real disturbed crazies they'd drug up, then they become spaaa-cey, rather than crazy. Spaaaa-cey and addicted. He'd seen it. In clean, out an addict. He, Richie, wasn't crazy, wasn't on meds, he was okay, more than okay, wanted to stay that way, stay just like that.

This guy, this Jew, looked strange, but he wasn't crazy. What was crazy was the cold in this cell, dark, damp, bone-chilling cold. Creeps into your joints and liver and intestines, gives you the creeps, and the cramps. Less than an hour after the door locked behind him, Richie already knew he wasn't doing well here. He wasn't doing well even before he checked in, so he had no good reserves to draw on, not a good situation. Don't let you bring nothing with you into prison, but with some grace, you come in with some reserved strength and health. Richie had nothing good coming in, this time. Came in with chills, and now he had shivers, and it was getting worse.

So here he was, with chills, shivers, teeth could chatter, too, in this cold, in with this Jew with the beard and his books and his prayers. That's what that mumbling was, it was praying, that's what that shawl thing was with the fringes, it was for praying, too, and those black boxes he strapped on to his arms and his head—scary that, majestic-scary—scare out the devil?—anyway prayer equipment, too. Richie stayed away from devil things, stayed away from church things, could be devils were lots of places, but here, when that Jew prayed, Richie felt that devils, wherever they were, weren't here. Was polite, that Jew, greeted Richie every morning, with soft speech. Didn't look like a prisoner, or speak like one, for sure not one who was sentenced for twenty-seven years.

How long had this guy been in the system?

Long enough to know about the *shu*?

Richi was coughing, trying not to spit too much. Didn't want no one to hear him coughing and spitting and shivering. If they'd see him sick and contagious they'd put him in isolation, in the *shu—secure housing unit*—meant isolation. That was the worst. A man could die there, alone in the shu!

Any normal inmate would rat to an authority that his cellmate was contagious. And the authorities would take the sick man out and isolate him in the shu. Every time the authorities passed by, Richie shivered under his sheet. Shivering from chills and from fear. Fear that he'd be reported, fear of the shu.

The bearded Jew didn't report him. The bearded Jew helped him drink some water. The bearded Jew even prayed for him.

Richie lived to tell the story. And to bless the bearded Jew.

Chapter Twelve
LEAH

Sholom was moved to upstate New York. Leah and the children moved as well. Leah continues to visit Sholom at the prison, visiting hours permitting. She waits with trust, prays with faith, that with G-d's help, the *habeas corpus* appeal, to be adjudicated by Judge Linda Reade, will free him. A Torah scroll was written in Sholom's honor. When it was all but completed, the prison was notified and asked: Could a group be sent up to Sholom, so that he himself could write the last letters of the Torah?

Permission was granted.

A *minyan*, ten men, prepared for the journey, including a Torah scribe, and two popular singers, Yaakov Shwekey and Boruch Levine.

Leah knew that when a prisoner is taken from his cell, he is in a different world. She imagined Sholom entering the meeting room, seeing the Torah scroll and the men who accompanied it. How he would smile when he greeted his visitors. They would see him holding his tattered copy of *Duties of the Heart*. His face would radiate faith.

Boruch Levine later enthused: "When we walked in, the bleak meeting room was transformed to a palace of joy. Sholom inked in the last letters. Yaakov Shwekey never sang his hit song *Rachem (Mercy)* with such passion. When I sang V'*zakani (Merit Me)* it never came from so deep a place. The walls could have melted.

"The prison was permeated with hope and yearning and the presence of the One Above. Everyone danced.

"When only ten minutes remained, Sholom stopped the music. He asked us to daven mincha with him. For so long he had not been able to doven with a minyan.

"The scribe handed him a white gown, a *kittel*, which is worn on Pesach and Yom Kippur. The davening was like the davening, of *neila*, the last prayers, before the gates are closed on Yom Kippur.

"Then we had to leave Sholom. Alone.

"We only wished that we would soon be able to dance together again, G-d willing, in Jerusalem..."

Epilogue:
WHERE ARE THE WOMEN NOW?

AIDEL

Aidel, yet hoping that Frank would convert, talked it over with Julie, a new friend who was herself in the process of converting to Judaism. Aidel asked her what motivates the convert. Was there any hope for Frank?

"I love my family," said Julie. "But I always felt different. I knew from when I was a teenager that I wanted to be a Jew. I just looked in the Bible, I mean the Old Testament, and did the best I could. Finally, after a number of years of study I was ready. I made the move to a religious community in New York."

"Frank isn't searching," said Aidel, "He likes his life the way it is."

"Well, if he wants it, don't you worry, Aidel. He'll come get it."

So far he had not. He was happy being a Noahide. He continued to appreciate Judaism, for his children, for his wife. But for himself?

In time, Aidel understood there was no hope of continuing the marriage, as painful as it was to part. Aidel told her story to many audiences, brought tears to many eyes and a determination to many hearts to "marry Jewish." She devoted herself to teaching preschool in Long Island. A year later, a beautiful and appropriate match was proposed for her.

Aidel and Isaac now live happily in Brooklyn, New York. Frank, too, is happily remarried.

Mona

Mona did use her knowledge and experience to help, encourage and counsel others. She wrote, she spoke, and she began to receive anonymous calls from distressed young mothers-to-be. Every person is a world, our sages tell us, and Mona considers it her calling to help and save many worlds.

Rachelle

She's down to a 16W! She joined an Overeaters Anonymous group, feels better, has more breath for dancing at her children's weddings. She uses her brain power to overcome cravings, and is grateful for her new life. Even Dr. Schiff commends her!

Reva

With always a good word about thanking the Master of the Universe, Reva continues teaching, publishing and lecturing. On a recent trip to Israel, she was encouraged to visit and pray at Amuka. Of course she continues to be there for her children, once a mother, always a mother. And grandchildren! As one granddaughter put it, "The world is her classroom!" And she continues her daily swim, on her favorite stretch of secret beach.

Tamar

Tamar enjoys Abigail and Benny's beautiful family. Benny is learning in a post-graduate yeshiva in Jerusalem, where he, Abigail and their young family live. Little did Tamar dream that her prayers would be answered so well! Abigail has a dedicated room for Tamar, who is a welcome and frequent visitor.

SHAINA

Shaina hopes that the story of her aunt will encourage others to opt for a Jewish burial. Better yet, she hopes for resurrection of the dead, so that even burial will no longer be necessary.

SARAH

Sarah is keeping up with her family and friends and her Tuesday Lunch and Learn, of course, plus her Monday spot on Ora's Teleconference. And she is a frequent guest speaker for women's groups in Brooklyn and Monsey, New York. Her face is public. Her heart is constantly praying for the salvation of her brother, Sholom Mordechai HaLevi ben Rivka.

LEAH

Leah knows that we are in the end of days, the last days before the final redemption. A new political climate – perhaps this will be G-d's agent to release Sholom. However it will happen, she has total faith and trust that it *will* happen. In fact, she has already selected the party hall, where hundreds of dear friends will come to celebrate his release. She has the perfect outfit assembled in her closet, ready at a moment's notice for the immediate thanksgiving celebration.

> *"She is clothed in strength and majesty*
> *And she will laugh on the last day."*
> -Aishet Chayil, Mishlei

Sarah's Notes
Themes of Exile and Redemption
In the Book of Exodus:

Egyptian Exile—prototype of all exiles.

Egyptian Redemption—prototype of all redemptions, in the merit of the righteous women, who never lost faith that they would be redeemed. They encouraged their husbands, raised families who hoped for and anticipated redemption.

Facets of Current Exile

Geographically: people separated from the Promised Land.

Psychologically: the challenge to maintain our holy heritage despite conflicting secular influences.

Consciousness: the longing for Divine Connection is misdirected into other longings.

Personal exile: Jewish nation-hood began in the crucible of Egyptian slavery. In subsequent exiles: isolation, Jews scattered among nations; Holy Temple destroyed, until in the Generation of the Redemption, we don't perceive what it is to be a Jew, not aware of our essential link to Divinity—our innate unparalleled connection to G-d, and our lifeline of Torah.

Universally: Hunger, war, illness, betrayals, confusion, political turmoil, disasters.

Cosmically: Divine withdrawal, G-d "hides" behind "laws" of nature. Holiness is not perceived.

Mystically: "Fallen sparks" must be elevated. Evil prevails.

Facets of Transition:

Geographically—longing for homeland, some return.

Psychologically- struggle to acquire tools to gain positive, holy, thoughts and emotions.

Consciousness—Growing desire for G-d, to keep and study His laws (Torah).

Personal: A time for gaining merit through returning to a Torah-inspired G-dly life.

Nationally: Growing awareness of the Messianic era, when the Holy Temple will be rebuilt in Jerusalem.

Universally: Awareness of Divine Providence. Earthquakes, tsunamis, floods, hurricanes, tornados, volcanoes, hint "naturally" (in unnatural frequencies) G-d's power. Goodness and Kindness Movement.

Cosmically: Divine withdrawal becomes prelude to Divine Intimacy. Mystically: "Sparks" are elevated. Evil makes vicious last efforts.

> "They shall beat their sword into plowshares, And their spear into pruning hooks." Isaiah

Is part of the transition, which we are experiencing now.

Facets of Redemption

Geographically: All Jews return to the Land of Israel.

Psychologically: only positive, G-dly, emotions and thoughts.

Consciousness: Infusion of Divinity, Divine empowerment.

Personal: New depth of appreciation of the Torah and Mitzvot. Personal fulfillment on all levels, all talent joyfully developed and used to connect self and others with G-d.

Nationally: Building of Third Holy Temple, new era of Torah study leading to Divine intimacy.

Universally: Era of health, peace, justice, prosperity.

Cosmically: Prevalence of Divine Consciousness. National leaders universally recognize and seek leadership from an extraordinary, wise and G-dly individual, seeped in Torah wisdom, known as Moshiach, (Messiah), the redeemer of all mankind. This leads to a new era, the era of Resurrection, *Techias Ha'meisim*, where death is banished, and the departed return to life.

Mystically: Evil is abolished. G-dly service involves continually increasing ones level of Divine consciousness and relationship with the Creator.

We are now living in the "end of days,"
the time of personal and cosmic redemption,
the time of the final redemption,
an era when the earth will be filled with the knowledge of G-d
as water covers the ocean floor.

***

ABOUT THE AUTHORS

Rivka Zakutinsky, lecturer, author, educator, and founder of Aura Press, a religious book imprint, holds a teaching degree from Beth Jacob Seminary in Brooklyn and a graduate degree from Hofstra University. She translated the classic *Techinas: Voice from the Heart* (Aura Press, 1992), and has authored *Finding the Woman of Valor* (Aura Press, 1996) and other books of interest to Jewish women. She lives in Brooklyn, New York.

Mrs. Zakutinsky can be reached at Ruthzakutinsky@gmail.com.

Yaffa Leba Gottlieb learned at Neve Yerushalayim Seminary in Jerusalem, and Machon Chana Institute in Crown Heights, after graduating from the University of Michigan and Washington University. A pioneer in breaking down barriers that isolated special needs people, she has also authored numerous children's books including the popular Charley Buttons book series. She lives with her husband and children in Crown Heights, New York.

Mrs. Gottlieb's can be reached at Yaffagottlieb@gmail.com. You can view her website www.yaffalebabooks.com.

Rivka and Yaffa co-authored *Around Sarah's Table*, (Free Press, 2001).

Made in the USA
Middletown, DE
27 August 2017